I0960666

The **HOUSING BOOM**

and **BUST**

THOMAS SOWELL

BASIC
BOOKS

A Member of the Perseus Books Group
New York

Copyright © 2009 by Thomas Sowell
Published by Basic Books,
A Member of the Perseus Books Group

Books published by Basic Books are available at special
discounts for bulk purchases in the United States by
corporations, institutions, and other organizations.
For more information, please contact the Special
Markets Department at the Perseus Books Group,
2300 Chestnut Street, Suite 200, Philadelphia, PA 19103,
or call (800) 810-4145, ext. 5000,
or e-mail special.markets@perseusbooks.com.

A CIP catalog record for this book is available
from the Library of Congress.

LCCN: 2009925585
ISBN: 978-0-465-01880-2

10 9 8 7 6 5 4 3 2 1

CONTENTS

PREFACE

Scary headlines and scarier statistics tell the story of a financial crisis on a scale not seen in decades— certainly not within the lifetime of most Americans. Moreover, this is a worldwide financial crisis. Financial institutions on both sides of the Atlantic have either collapsed or have been saved from collapse by government bailouts, as a result of buying securities based on American housing values that eroded or evaporated.

This financial tsunami has been followed by a political flood of rhetoric, accompanied by finger-pointing in all directions. Who was really responsible? What set this off?

There was no single, dramatic event that set this off, the way the assassination of the Archduke Ferdinand set off the chain of events that led to the First World War or the way the arrest of political operatives committing burglary at the Watergate Hotel led to the resignation of President Richard Nixon. A whole series of very questionable decisions by many people, in many places, over a period of years, built up the pressures that led to a sudden collapse of the housing market and of financial institutions that began to fall like dominoes as a result of investing in securities based on housing prices.

This book is designed to unravel the tangled threads of that story. It also attempts to determine whether what is being done to deal with the problem is more likely to make things better or worse.

Thomas Sowell
Hoover Institution
Stanford University

ACKNOWLEDGMENTS

As with many of my other books, this book owes much to my two dedicated research assistants, Na Liu and Elizabeth Costa. In addition to their ferreting out and sifting through vast amounts of reading material to find the things that were relevant to this study, Ms. Costa has done the copy-editing and fact-checking, while Ms. Liu has converted my ancient WordPerfect 5.1 word-processing files into the much more complex Quark files from which this book has been directly printed. I am grateful to them both and to the Hoover Institution whose generosity has made possible the work that we all do.

Chapter 1

The Economics of the Housing Boom

Few markets have had such a skyrocketing rise, followed immediately by an equally steep plummet to new depths, as the housing market has had in the early years of the twenty-first century. From 2000 to 2005, the median sales price of American single-family homes rose by one-third, from $143,600 to $219,600. In some places, the rise was even sharper. Over those same years, the median home price in New York rose 79 percent, in Los Angeles 110 percent and in San Diego 127 percent. In coastal California, the rise was especially sharp— and so was the later fall.

Who or what caused the housing boom and bust?

There was no single cause of the housing crisis, and there is certainly plenty of blame to go around, especially among Washington politicians of both parties, who are strenuously looking for villains outside of Washington. During the housing boom there were some voices of sanity that warned against the risky way things were being done, both in Washington and in Wall Street. However, during that boom, warnings were brushed aside with clever phrases or with pious statements about the benefits of increased home ownership.

When trying to get at the causes of any major social phenomenon, we are likely to find that these causes range across a wide spectrum. The causes of the housing boom and bust have been as general as the flaws and shortcomings of human beings and as specific as the effects of Federal Reserve System policy on interest rates or a change in mortgage loan eligibility standards by the Federal National Mortgage Association ("Fannie Mae") or the Federal Home Loan Mortgage Corporation ("Freddie Mac"). The housing market is greatly affected by interest rates and credit eligibility rules, but there is much more to the story than that.

The record-breaking housing price rises that preceded the record-breaking housing market collapse were not evenly spread across the United States but were heavily concentrated in a relatively few places. Much confusion between local trends and national trends in housing markets contributed to counterproductive government policies. We need to understand what led to both kinds of home price trends during the boom before examining the causes and consequences of the housing bust— and the repercussions that spread, not only across the nation but internationally.

THE CAST OF CHARACTERS

In order to follow the story of the housing boom and bust more easily, it may be worth pausing to briefly note the main cast of characters in the housing markets. While the individual home buyer may deal solely with a bank that provides the money to buy the house, in exchange for a mortgage to be paid off in monthly installments, behind that bank and over that bank are all sorts of other institutions, whose actions affect or control the housing markets.

The Federal Reserve System has a general authority to regulate banks across the country, as well as specific powers to take actions which affect interest rates and the money supply. Given the great importance of the level of interest rates in the home mortgage markets, the Federal Reserve is a major player in that market, even though that is just one of the markets in which its influence is felt.

The Federal National Mortgage Association (*Fannie Mae*) and the Federal Home Loan Mortgage Corporation (*Freddie Mac*) are two government-created, but privately owned, profit-making enterprises that buy mortgages from banks. By selling these mortgages, banks get money from a 30-year mortgage without having to wait 30 years for monthly payments from home buyers to pay off their debts. With the proceeds from these sales to Fannie Mae or Freddie Mac, or to other financial institutions, the banks then have money to lend again to create more mortgages from which to profit.

More than two-thirds of the mortgages made in 2004, for example, were resold to some other financial institution, including Fannie Mae and Freddie Mac. These two government-sponsored enterprises bought more than one-third of all the mortgages in the nation that were resold by the original lenders. In order to qualify to sell their mortgages to Fannie Mae or Freddie Mac, banks must conform to the rules and standards prescribed by these mortgage market giants, including rules and standards that banks must in turn apply to people who seek loans to buy houses. One of the consequences, however, of reselling mortgages on a large scale is that the initial lender has fewer incentives to be meticulous about the financial qualifications of the people to whom mortgage loans are made.

The U.S. Department of Housing and Urban Development (*HUD*) is another major institution in the housing market. HUD exercises authority over Fannie Mae and Freddie Mac, and therefore indirectly over banks and home buyers, as well as directly influencing mortgage lending practices.

Other important players— and relatively new players in recent years— are Wall Street firms which buy mortgages, bundle them together and issue stocks and bonds based on the value of those mortgages. Wall Street firms have sold these bundles to investors across the country and around the world. Although a California home buyer might borrow the money from a local bank to buy a house, the ultimate source of that money might be in New York or London or Tokyo.

These and other organizations affecting the housing market are very different from one another and are responsible to very different constituencies. The Department of Housing and Urban Development (HUD) is a Cabinet-level agency responsible to whatever administration is in power in Washington. Although the Federal Reserve System is also a government agency, it is led by a board whose members' staggered terms in office overlap different administrations, in order to make them independent of any particular administration.

Fannie Mae and Freddie Mac are responsible to their stockholders, as Wall Street firms are. But Fannie Mae and Freddie Mac are also what are called "government-sponsored enterprises"— meaning that they were created by the federal government, which has some continuing involvement in their policies. More important, that government involvement leads other financial institutions to lend to these two hybrid institutions at lower interest rates than they would to completely private enterprises, because of the implicit assumption that, in the event of a crisis, the federal government would not let Fannie Mae or Freddie Mac fail.

Investors buy securities issued by these two government-sponsored enterprises with the same reliance on a federal guarantee that is nowhere explicit but is widely assumed to exist de facto anyway. As the *Wall Street Journal* put it: "Their profit is privatized but their risk is socialized."

What all this means is that, with such very different organizations having a major influence on the housing markets, there is no inherent reason to expect them to coordinate their actions, so as to produce some consistent policy in those markets. They each have their own incentives, their own agendas and their own constituencies.

Other organizations of various sorts can also play a role in the housing markets, including in some cases the U.S. Department of Justice, as we shall see in Chapter 4. But, for now, the organizations just described can be considered the main players.

THE COST OF HOUSING

Housing is special in a number of ways. It is special to homeowners, for most of whom their house is their largest financial asset and, at the same time, their greatest financial liability. Census data show that home equity— the value of the home, over and above what is owed on the mortgage— is by far the largest single asset in the average household, accounting for 42 percent of the household's total net worth. Meanwhile, a study by the Federal Reserve System found that mortgage debt was 82 percent of the total debt of homeowners.

Whether people are buying or renting, monthly housing costs are often also the largest single item in their current budgets. In some places with especially high housing prices, such as parts of coastal California, either rent or monthly mortgage payments have taken one-half of the average person's income. An extreme example is Salinas, California, where the monthly mortgage payment on a median priced house has taken 60 percent of new home buyers' median income. That of course severely limits what kind of standard of living home buyers can afford with what is left.

Interest Rates

Housing is also special because a house is something that can seldom be bought and paid for immediately in cash. Because borrowed money is what usually pays for houses, the interest rate on that borrowed money is crucial— and that interest rate varies greatly with circumstances in the economy as a whole, in addition to varying considerably over time and from one borrower to another. While some factors affect housing prices in local areas, other factors operate nationwide. Interest rates are set nationwide by the Federal Reserve System, through the interest rate it charges to lenders, who in turn lend to the general public, including people buying homes.

The interest rate on a conventional 30-year mortgage was about 8 percent in 1973, 18 percent in 1981 and 6 percent in 2005. At any given time, the interest rate also varies from person to person, depending on the financial condition and credit record of each individual. Those individuals whose credit ratings are below par may be denied loans at the prevailing interest rates, but granted "subprime" loans, which charge higher interest rates to offset the greater risk of lending to people who have lower incomes or a history of credit problems.

In general, not only are people with lower credit scores charged higher interest rates for mortgage loans, people charged higher interest have higher rates of late payments or foreclosures, suggesting that the market has accurately assessed the risks. All this means that the cost of buying a given house can vary greatly with the times, with the individual and with the various "creative"— and risky—

ways of trying to make the monthly mortgage payments affordable, especially in markets with high home prices.

Just a difference of a percentage point or two can significantly change the cost of buying a home. When buying a house by taking out a 30-year mortgage for $400,000, the monthly payment will be less than $2,200 when the interest rate is 5 percent, but more than $2,600 when the interest rate is 7 percent. That is a difference of more than $5,000 a year— 5,000 *after tax* dollars.

Another way of saying the same thing is that a monthly mortgage payment that would cover the cost of a 30-year mortgage for $400,000 when the interest rate is 7 percent would cover a 30-year mortgage of nearly $500,000 when the interest rate is 5 percent. In short, declining interest rates not only enable more people to be able to afford to buy a house, they enable the same person to buy a more expensive house without a higher monthly mortgage payment. In both cases, lower interest rates increase the demand for housing and thereby drive up home prices.

During the early years of the twenty-first century, the interest rates that the Federal Reserve System charged financial institutions were brought down to extremely low levels. Competition among financial institutions in turn brought down the interest rates they charged, including interest rates on mortgage loans. Mortgage interest rates fell to their lowest level in decades. Not surprisingly, housing prices rose to record high levels. This helped set the stage for the housing boom.

Down Payments

One of the biggest hurdles to becoming a homeowner has been the traditional substantial down payment required— often 20 percent of the price of a home. That has been an especially large hurdle where home prices are highest. People who already have a home can often sell that home, even if it is not yet paid for, paying off the mortgage from the sale price and using the money left over— their equity in the house— as a down payment for a new house. That has usually been the primary source of a down payment for California homeowners buying another home, their savings usually being secondary. But, after the housing boom turned to bust, savings became the primary source of down payments in California, as homes no longer sold as fast or for as much money as before.

People who are buying a home for the first time, however, have had to come up with the hard cash, which many found difficult or impossible— again, especially in places with very expensive housing. While first-time home buyers were about half of all home buyers in California in the mid-1990s, that proportion fell to about a third during the housing boom in the early years of the twenty-first century. Down payments from first-time buyers in California were much less than down payments from repeat buyers— less than $30,000 compared to more than $100,000 for repeat buyers in 2008, for example.

Lenders are, of course, well aware that requiring substantial down payments limits the number of people who can afford mortgage loans— and therefore limits the total amount of business they can do and the profit to be made from making mortgage loans. Obviously, there must be some offsetting advantage to having such a requirement. That advantage is reducing the risk of default. A home buyer with a substantial investment in the home from the outset is less likely to someday simply walk away from the mortgage and the house, leaving the lender in the lurch.

In exceptionally expensive housing markets, first-time buyers have had to pay an especially high proportion of their incomes for monthly mortgage payments, since they have often made the minimum down payment possible. First-time buyers have also more often than others resorted to various "creative"— and risky— methods of financing the purchase of a home.

EXPENSIVE HOUSING MARKETS

Although the housing boom and bust, and its financial repercussions, have been national and even international in their scope, many of the problems that provided the impetus for these economic disasters were local in origin. The national and even international market for local mortgages has meant that the repercussions of housing crises in various localities can spread far beyond those localities. Moreover, a confusion between the local and the nationwide availability of "affordable housing" has contributed to government policies that led to the boom and bust. To understand all this, we need to start at square one, the scattered localities around the country where housing prices have been some multiple of the national average, and were rising much faster than the national average, during the housing boom.

California— and especially coastal California— has been the largest of these exceptionally expensive housing markets. It has also been the most expensive and with the fastest rising home prices. At the height of the housing boom in 2005, the top ten areas with the biggest home price increases over the previous five years were all in California. Yet California home prices were once very similar to home prices in the rest of the nation. It was only after the decade of the 1970s that home prices in much of coastal California became far higher than home prices in the country as a whole.

In the San Francisco Bay Area, for example, the median-priced home in 2005 cost more than three times the national average. In the city of San Francisco, the median home sales price that year was $765,000. In March of the same year, home prices in San Mateo County (adjacent to San Francisco) rose at a rate of $2,000 *a day* and later peaked at just over one million dollars in 2007. This price was paid for homes averaging less than 2,000 square feet.

San Mateo was by no means unique among California communities in having modest-sized houses that were selling for what would be charged for large luxury homes elsewhere. For the state as a whole, including its interior valleys where housing prices were lower, the median sales price of homes peaked at $561,000 in 2006, when the median size of the houses sold was 1,600 square feet. Most Californians were not living in mansions, but many were paying what would be mansion prices, in some other places, for modest middle class homes.

Although the housing boom and bust is a national problem in terms of its repercussions, its origins tended to be concentrated in particular places with unusually high housing prices and unusually volatile changes in those prices. For example, while home prices rose 13 percent nationwide in a single year, from 2004 to 2005, the range was from a 4 percent rise in Michigan to a 35 percent rise in Arizona. As already noted, California housing prices have long been some multiple of prices in the country as a whole.

What is different about such places?

Certainly the cost of building a house does not vary anywhere nearly as drastically as the prices of houses in different places. Nor does the quality of the houses vary that much between the high-priced states and the lower-priced states. Although San Francisco has some of the highest home prices and apartment rents in the country, the houses are often rather modest and built close together. As for apartments, the *San Francisco Chronicle* mentioned a graduate student looking for a place to rent in San Francisco, who was "visiting one exorbitantly priced hovel after another."

Conceivably, rising incomes or rising populations might explain why some places have higher or faster rising housing prices than others. But, in fact, incomes were rising *less* in California than in the rest of the country during the decade of the 1970s, when California housing prices became a multiple of the national average. Nor have population increases usually been what has driven home prices up in some places so much faster than the national average. Population increase on the San Francisco peninsula during the 1970s was virtually identical with population increases nationally— 11.9 percent versus 11.5 percent, respectively. Housing prices in Palo Alto, California (near Stanford University), nearly quadrupled during the decade of the 1970s, when that community's population actually declined by 8 percent.

What then does distinguish the places with skyrocketing housing prices from other places?

Studies of housing prices show that what varies drastically from one place to another is the price of the *land* on which houses are built. In areas with very high housing prices, the cost of the land is often some *multiple* of the cost of building the house. Economists at the National Bureau of Economic Research estimated that the cost of a quarter-acre lot added about $140,000 to the price of a house in Chicago, over and above the cost of constructing the house itself. In San Diego, a quarter-acre lot added about $285,000 to the cost of the house itself, in New York City the same size lot added about $350,000, and in San Francisco nearly $700,000. The extraordinary cost of the land in San

Francisco helps explain why modest but very expensive homes in that city are often jammed close together.*

While great variations in the price of land from one place to another help answer some questions, these variations raise other questions. Why are there such great variations in the price of land from one place to another, in the first place? Moreover, why did the price of housing suddenly become radically more expensive in California in the 1970s, when it was not before? Surely the amount of land in California did not change radically during that decade.

In a sense it did. It changed politically.

The decade of the 1970s saw a rapid spread of laws and policies in California severely restricting the use of land.** Often these laws and policies forbade the building of anything on vast areas of land, in the name of preserving "open space," "saving farmland," "protecting the environment," "historical preservation" and other politically attractive slogans. Moreover, these restrictions were extended to more and more land over the years.

The normal transfer of land from one use to another over time was often stopped by such laws and policies, so that a farmer who quit farming was not allowed to sell the land to someone who might build houses on the site. Instead, the

---

*For a graphic example, see the photograph on page 58 of the article titled "Is This House Worth $1.2 Million?" in the October 28, 2002 issue of *Fortune* magazine.

**Amazingly, some supposedly sophisticated people apparently believe that there is an actual physical shortage of land in places with high housing prices: "Those areas already are crowded," a *Wall Street Journal* reporter said, even though more than half of San Mateo County, California, for example, consists of open space and similar land use restrictions are common in other communities with extremely high housing prices. The comment is from James R. Hagerty, "After Big Run-Up in Real Estate, Some on Coasts Are Cashing Out," *Wall Street Journal*, September 22, 2004, pp. A1 ff.

former farmland could be forced to become "open space" by various restrictions placed on its use. In this and other ways, large and growing amounts of land in many coastal California communities became "open space"— more than half of all the land in San Mateo County, for example. This artificial scarcity of land of course drove up the price of the remaining land in the county, creating the conditions in which modest-sized homes became literally million-dollar homes in that county.

While California was different from most of the rest of the country in the extent and severity of its land use restrictions, it was not unique. The same kinds of land-use restrictions which spread through many coastal California communities during the 1970s spread through various other places around the country, either during that decade or in other years. But, in whatever years building restrictions were tightened in various localities, those were usually the same years in which housing prices skyrocketed.

A study of the dates that marked the takeoff of home prices in various communities across the country found that those times "in which housing markets became unaffordable closely followed the approval of state growth-management laws or restrictive local plans." An international study of urban areas around the world with "severely unaffordable" housing likewise found that 23 out of 26 such areas had strong "smart-growth" policies. The consequences contrast painfully with the self-congratulatory phrase. As a former governor of the Reserve Bank of New Zealand put it, in another international study of home prices, "the affordability of housing is overwhelmingly a function of just one thing, the extent to which governments place artificial restrictions on the supply of residential land."

In addition to prohibitions on building, land use restrictions in some places have also taken the form of requiring that each home be built on a lot no smaller than an acre, or several acres, in contrast to the usual middle-class home on a quarter-acre lot. Loudoun County, Virginia, for example, enacted laws in 2001 which restricted the building of homes to one house per 10 acres in some places, 20 acres in others and 50 acres in still others. Fayette County, Kentucky, has set minimum lot sizes at forty acres.

Minimum lot-size laws ensure that the land costs of building a house will be vastly greater than otherwise, and housing costs correspondingly beyond the reach of most Americans. It is a way of surrounding upscale communities with a wide buffer zone, keeping less affluent people at bay. The resulting high costs of housing do not adversely affect homeowners already living in the upscale community. Most of these existing homeowners either have mortgages negotiated before the land use restrictions were enacted or else own their homes outright. In either case, the values of their homes shoot up after the restrictions, so that they gain financially as well as by keeping out less affluent people and thereby preserving the character of the community as they like it.

Because these were usually local laws and policies restricting building, such restrictions have not been uniform across the country. Instead, there have been extremely expensive enclaves here and there with extremely restrictive land use laws, with most of the rest of the country having much more modest housing prices. A study of housing prices across the nation concluded:

> Today, a family in an American city without growth-management planning can buy a very nice "middle-manager's" home, with about 2,200 square feet, four bedrooms, two-and-one-half baths, and a two-car garage, for $150,000 to $200,000. In cities that have had growth-management planning for ten to fifteen years, that same home costs $300,000 to $400,000. In cities that have had it

for twenty-five years or more, the same house costs from $500,000 to as much as $1.5 million.

These estimates are consistent with estimates made by the nationwide real estate company Coldwell Banker, comparing the price of the same house in Houston and San Jose. Houston has been a city at the opposite pole from places like San Jose, in terms of laws affecting the use of land. Houston has not even had zoning laws, much less the vast array of other constraints common in San Jose or other places with severe land use restrictions. Coldwell Banker has estimated that a house that costs $155,000 in Houston would cost more than a million dollars in San Jose.

Even rising incomes and growing populations in places without severe land use restrictions have seldom produced housing price increases at all comparable to those in places with severe land use restrictions. While housing prices skyrocketed in California during the 1970s, even though incomes in California were not rising as fast as incomes nationwide, in Houston incomes were rising *faster* than the national average and yet Houston continued to have some of the most affordable housing in the nation. Dallas likewise has long had family incomes above the national average and housing prices below the national average.

Open space laws are not the only laws or policies that drive up housing prices by restricting the building of houses. Among the arsenal of weapons available to those who want to prevent development are zoning laws, height restrictions, minimum lot size laws, historical preservation laws, building permit limits and farmland preservation laws. In some jurisdictions, planning commissions have arbitrary powers to grant or deny permission to build, which means that they can impose costs by requiring the builder to make whatever modifications they wish, at whatever costs these modifications might require, in addition to the accumulating costs of delay as more and more hearings are scheduled in a building approval process that can go on for years before permission is finally granted to actually begin building— if that permission ever comes.

In some communities, private citizens or groups can make objections to building plans, and the adjudications of such objections take more time, regardless of the merits or lack of merits of the objections. While these costs are initially imposed on the builder, those who buy or rent the housing can end up paying for all these things.

It is not only in the building of single-family homes that the presence or absence of these impediments affects the costs of housing, both directly and by preventing or discouraging housing from being built in the first place. Conversely, when and where there are few impediments to building, even a growing demand for housing can be met without forcing up prices the way they are forced up in more restrictive environments. In Manhattan during the 1950s, for example, tens of thousands of new housing units were built without apartment rents or condominium prices increasing in real terms— that is, money prices adjusted for inflation. But, in later years, after new building restrictions began to be imposed in the 1970s, a later study found "skyrocketing prices" (in real terms) in Manhattan, while the total housing stock there increased by less than 10 percent in a quarter of a century.

It was much the same story in Las Vegas, where the population almost tripled between 1980 and 2000, but the median price of housing did not change in real terms, that is, correcting for inflation. However, since 90 percent of the land in Nevada is owned by the federal government, the supply of land for building depends on the government's willingness to continue to sell land to be developed. After environmentalist groups raised objections to such sales in the twenty-first century, land use restrictions were followed by rapidly rising housing prices in Las Vegas, as has happened elsewhere under such land use constraints.

Much of the impetus for severe land use restrictions comes from individuals and groups who create an impression that they are trying to prevent the last few patches of greenery from being paved over. In reality, less than 10 percent of the land area of the United States has been developed. Trees alone cover more than six times the area of all the cities and towns in the country put together. But, for political decision-making, impressions can carry more weight than facts. As former Congressman Dick Armey put it: "Demagoguery beats data."

As housing prices rose from 2000 to 2005, this was widely conceived as a national problem, especially by Washington politicians seeking to create a national program to deal with it. However, the wide disparities in housing prices from community to community— even between coastal California and that state's inland valleys— show a very different picture. In 2005, the *New York Times* reported:

> Despite a widespread sense that real estate has never been more expensive, families in the vast majority of the country can still buy a house for a smaller share of their income than they could have a generation ago.
>
> A sharp fall in mortgage rates since the early 1980's, a decline in mortgage fees and a rise in incomes have more than made up for rising house prices in almost every place outside of New York, Washington, Miami and along the coast in California.

In other words, most of the country was *not* suffering from skyrocketing housing prices, which were largely confined to particular communities in which there were severe limitations on the building of housing. During the housing boom, home prices in the 10 most expensive metropolitan areas were more than twice as high as the national average. In these high-price enclaves, people buying a home for the first time— and therefore not having the equity in an existing home to use as a down payment— "often must spend more than half of their income on mortgage payments" in places like New York and Los Angeles, the *New York Times* reported. But the percentage of median family income required to buy a house in Tampa was 21 percent and in Dallas 13 percent. Dallas, like Houston, has relatively few building restrictions.

A fundamental misconception of the housing market existed both during the housing boom and after the bust. That misconception was that the free market failed to produce affordable housing, and that government intervention was therefore necessary, in order to enable ordinary people to find a place to live that was within their means. Yet the hard evidence points in the opposite direction. It has been precisely where there was massive government intervention, in the form of severe building restrictions, that housing prices skyrocketed. Where the market was more or less left alone— places like Houston and Dallas, for example— housing prices took a smaller share of family income than in the past.

In short, the problem of a lack of "affordable housing," as conceived by many in the media and in politics, bore little resemblance to the situation in the real world. It was not a national problem but a severe problem in particular places. Washington politicians who set out to solve a problem that they misconceived contributed instead to the housing boom and bust, as will become clear in the following chapters.

"CREATIVE" FINANCING

At extremely high prices for even modest homes in places like coastal California, home buyers were especially prone to resort to risky ways of financing their purchases, in order to be able to buy a home at all. Regarded as "creative" or "innovative" ways of coping with high housing prices, these methods of financing the purchase of homes spread, especially to other areas with very high housing prices.

Among the "creative" ways of financing a home purchase have been no-down-payment mortgages and mortgages on which only the interest is paid at first. Among the variations on interest-only loans, a common one has been making monthly mortgage payments covering only the interest for the first two years of a 30-year mortgage, followed by larger monthly payments over the next 28 years to pay off the loan itself. Interest-only mortgages were typically mortgages with interest rates that would also vary over time, according to what interest rates were in the economy at large. In other words, the monthly mortgage payments could go up, even during the first two years when only the interest on the loan was being paid, if interest rates in the economy as a whole went up.

Adjustable-rate mortgages— known as ARMs— had a number of variations. One of the more adventurous versions of the ARMs was one in which the home buyer had the option to pay less than the amount of the interest in some months during the interest-only period. While convenient for dealing with temporary financial problems, these option ARMs meant that paying less than the interest in some months meant that the unpaid interest was added to the principal, so that the home buyer who used that option could end up owing more than the original amount of the mortgage.

These various kinds of adjustable-rate mortgages, taken out when interest rates were unusually low, brought monthly mortgage payments down below what they would be in a conventional 30-year fixed-rate mortgage, thus enabling more people to stretch their incomes to cover the price of buying homes that they might otherwise be unable to afford.

ARMs were especially attractive methods of "creative financing" in places where housing was especially expensive. Thus, while housing prices were *rising* in the early years of the twenty-first century, initial monthly mortgage payments were *falling* from 2002 to 2004, as a result of what the *Wall Street Journal* called "the onslaught of creative mortgage products— from interest-only loans to adjustable-rate mortgages carrying starter rates as low as 1%— that have allowed buyers to keep initial payments down even as home prices have soared."

The traditional fixed-rate 30-year mortgages, which were once a majority of all mortgages, were no longer a majority during the housing boom, as ARMs and other "creative" ways of financing the purchase of a home grew rapidly to cope with soaring housing prices. Such innovative mortgages quickly went from being rare to becoming common, especially in places with very high housing costs.

In 2002, less than 10 percent of new mortgages in the United States were interest-only mortgages, but that rose to 31 percent by 2005, as home prices rose. In a number of California cities, as well as in Denver, Washington, Phoenix and Seattle, interest-only loans were 40 percent of all mortgage loans made in 2005. In the San Francisco Bay Area, interest-only loans rose from being 11 percent of all new mortgages in 2002 to becoming 66 percent of all new mortgages in 2005, the height of the housing boom, in an area with some of the most expensive real estate in the country.

Such arrangements were especially attractive to people who expected their incomes to increase over time. By the time the higher monthly payments would become due, in order to begin paying off the principal, the borrowers' rising incomes would enable them to afford those higher payments— *if* all worked out according to plan.

There was yet another reason for borrowers to take on risky "creative" financial arrangements during a housing boom. With housing prices rising substantially from year to year, home buyers could begin acquiring equity in their homes, even before time came for them to start paying off the principal on their mortgage loans.

For example, imagine someone buying a home in one of the places with booming housing prices, by taking out a no-down payment loan and a $600,000 mortgage, in which only the interest is paid during the first two years. Even if the home buyer turns out to be unable to make the larger monthly mortgage payments when these higher payments are scheduled to begin after the initial two years of interest-only payments are over, the increased value of the house in a rising housing market could enable the buyer to leave with considerable money, even if it was impossible for the buyer to continue living in the home after the monthly payments rose to an unaffordable level. If the house that initially cost $600,000 increased in value to $800,000 in the meantime, then the home buyer could sell the house for $800,000, paying off the $600,000 mortgage in order to do so, and walk away with $200,000 in cash.

Such scenarios became common during the housing boom, especially in the high-price enclaves, where home prices were skyrocketing. The only thing unrealistic about this example is that a $600,000 home would have to be a *very* modest home— if not a "fixer-upper"— in some coastal California communities during the housing boom. In other words, the gains to be made in such places were likely to be even greater than in this example.

This was just one of the ways in which the rising value of houses could be turned into ready cash during the housing boom. Home equity loans also became common during the boom, whether the home was owned outright or the buyer was still making mortgage payments. For homes bought and paid for before the housing boom, the amount of money that could be borrowed, based on the house's rising value during the boom, could easily exceed the total amount paid for the house. For example, a Chicago man bought a 100-year-old house for $90,000 in 1992 and, during the housing boom, took out a $200,000 home equity loan on that house, which was now worth about $700,000.

In more expensive housing markets and over longer periods of time, the situation could get even more extreme. In Oakland, California, a couple bought a two-bedroom bungalow back in 1954 for $11,500. It was refinanced several times over the years by their children and, in the end, was lost to foreclosure with the family owing more than $450,000 for the money they had borrowed on that home.

Income tax rules also made borrowing against a home's equity attractive. Because mortgage interest payments can be deducted for income tax purposes, the interest paid on home equity loans could also be deducted, although interest on credit card debt or other debt was not deductible. Therefore it often paid anyone with any other kind of debt to pay off that debt with a home equity loan, whose interest would be deductible for income tax purposes. More and more people began to do this during the housing boom. In 2003, home equity loans totaled $593 billion. Such loans soared during the housing boom, nearly doubling to $1.13 trillion in 2007.

A special variation on the home equity loan was what was called "cash-out refinancing." Someone owing $300,000 on a mortgage with a fixed interest rate of 8 percent could take out a new loan to replace the old loan when the interest rate fell to 6 percent. But instead of taking out another $300,000 mortgage loan at 6 percent, the homeowner could take out a $400,000 mortgage loan at 6 percent, paying off the existing loan from the proceeds of the new loan and keeping $100,000 in cash. In an era of rising home prices, lenders were often quite willing to lend more money on a house that now had a higher market value. For the borrower, refinancing at a lower interest rate could mean that the monthly mortgage payment would not increase, even with a larger mortgage. These kinds of home-equity loans increased more than ten-fold during the housing boom, rising from $26 billion in 2000 to $318 billion in 2006. As of 2006, 86 percent of all home mortgage refinances were "cash-out" refinances.

Many home equity loans for the elderly did not require any repayment at all by the borrower, but simply transferred part of the equity to the lender, who could turn that equity into cash after the death of the borrower. These "reverse mortgages," as they were called, also increased greatly during the housing boom. There were fewer than 8,000 reverse mortgages in 2001 but the number soared to more than 40,000 in 2005.

Given all the ways of tapping the equity in a home to take out hard cash, it should not be surprising that the average equity in a home, which was 86 percent of its value back in 1945, was just 55 percent of its value in 2003.

There were many incentives to buy houses in a rising market, including buying for the purpose of re-selling at a higher price, even if the buyer never intended to live in the house, or bought several houses on credit at the same time, speculating on future appreciation. Such speculations in turn contributed to the demand for housing, with a resulting continuation of home price increases. Low initial interest rates, and the resulting low initial monthly mortgage payments, made speculation profitable in a rising housing market. By buying a house, or multiple houses, with low initial monthly mortgage payments and then selling them later for a higher price before the increased mortgage payments became due, many speculators could carry on very profitable speculations in very expensive houses with relatively little hard cash of their own.

Often speculators bought homes that needed fixing up or sprucing up and then quickly sold them— a process called "flipping." As *Money* magazine described the process:

> In hot spots like Las Vegas and Florida, real estate flippers have discovered that a modest down payment and a little patience can net them tens (even hundreds) of thousands of dollars in profits, sometimes tax-free. The most aggressive of them figure that some combo of paint, new flooring and kitchen upgrades can turn the dumpy house they bought for $300,000 in February into a $400,000 property they can unload in July. And in the most sizzling markets, they're absolutely right.

Fast turnarounds are not uncommon, as *Forbes* magazine reported:

> "It was disgusting," says Alan Washer. Grime coated the walls of the 1,600-square-foot, four-bedroom home; the musty air reeked of a cat colony that had played havoc with the wood floors. But one man's wreck is another guy's riches. Washer bought the house, in the leafy Chicago suburb of Oak Park, for $225,000 in July, spending an additional $5,000 to haul away heaps of rubbish left inside. Fixed up, he figured, it was worth $430,000. But two weeks after he closed on the place— and before he could refinish the floors or replace a rotting soffit or the old roof—

Washer got a call from someone offering $315,000. He took it.

With housing speculation, however, comes risk. If home prices merely level off, that can create serious problems for speculative home buyers— especially those owing money on multiple homes bought with mortgages whose monthly payments are scheduled to increase after the interest-only period is followed by the higher payments required to begin paying off the principal on the mortgages. If home prices fall, that can create even more serious problems for both home buyers in general and the financial institutions that lend to them.

Many people who were not professional speculators were nevertheless, in effect, speculating not only on home prices but also on their own incomes rising fast enough to be able to begin making larger monthly mortgage payments after the initial interest-only payments period had passed. Adjustable-rate mortgages meant that buyers were also speculating on how long interest rates would stay at historic lows and how fast they would rise afterwards. One of the inherent problems of speculation— whether in housing or elsewhere— is that the resulting prices during a boom bear no relationship to anything other than what people believe or hope. And once those beliefs or hopes change, for whatever reason, these prices can plummet.

KNOWLEDGE AND DECISIONS

In any aspect of life, regardless of how much or how little knowledge we have, we must make decisions. The housing market is no exception. Sometimes we can draw upon our own experience or depend on the knowledge of other people but, in some cases, no one is really very knowledgeable when new and untried things are involved, such as the exotic new financial arrangements growing out of the "creative" financing of home purchases that became increasingly common during the housing boom.

Because both low interest rates and lowered mortgage eligibility standards enabled many low-income people, sometimes less educated people, to buy houses who could not have done so in earlier years, some of the least knowledgeable and least experienced home buyers were now financing their purchases with some of the newest and most complicated mortgages. There are indications that many of these less sophisticated home buyers may not have fully understood how much their monthly payments could rise under adjustable rate mortgages with initially very low interest rates and sometimes an initial period of perhaps two years when they were paying only interest on their mortgage loan.

Sometimes the initial interest rates charged on interest-only loans were even below the current market interest rate. For example, if the prevailing interest rate on conventional mortgages was 6 percent, a so-called "teaser" rate of 4 percent might be charged for the first few months on a new mortgage, in order to attract people seeking to buy a home that was something of a stretch for someone with their income. The unusually low initial monthly mortgage payments, made possible by the temporary "teaser" rate, would then be followed by higher monthly mortgage payments when the prevailing interest rate replaced the teaser rate— followed still later by another increase in monthly mortgage when time came for payments to begin repaying the principal on the mortgage loan.

During the height of the housing boom in 2005 and 2006, an estimated 15 percent of adjustable-rate mortgages that were issued had initial interest rates *below two percent*. In short, within a very few years, monthly mortgage payments under such "creative" arrangements could rise far above their initial level under low introductory "teaser" interest rates. How many of those who signed up for such loans understood all this is a serious question.

For those buying houses for speculation, in order to sell them before the initial "teaser" rates rose, this could be a rational— and very profitable— arrangement. In California, for example, the median time that a home remained on the Multiple Listing Service before being sold was less than two weeks in 2004 and just over two weeks in 2005. During those two years, at least half of all homes on sale had multiple offers from prospective buyers. It was not uncommon in some California communities for the initial asking price to be bid up further, rather than compromised downward.

In this frenzied and booming market, "teaser" rate mortgages were a boon for speculators who could buy a house, perhaps fix it up or spruce it up, and sell it again very soon. Nationwide, a survey by the National Association of Realtors found that, during the housing boom, homes were bought as investments, rather than to live in, by 28 percent of home buyers in 2005 and by 22 percent of home buyers in 2006.

But for people buying a home to live in, low "teaser" rates could be a trap, if not understood. One study found that subprime borrowers "are disproportionately minority and lower income, older, less well educated, less financially sophisticated" people. However, getting in over their heads in complex adjustable-rate loans with initially low "teaser" rates may be more of a symptom, rather than a cause, of an unstable situation that could end in default and foreclosure. A study of adjustable-rate subprime home mortgage foreclosures found the great majority were foreclosed even before the interest rate rose.

At the other end of the knowledge scale, sophisticated financial firms like Moody's and Standard & Poor's, whose ratings of the relative risks of different kinds of investments were depended upon by Wall Street firms and investors around the world, had only a very limited amount of hard data available to use when making ratings of stocks and bonds that were based on new and exotic mortgages. As one financial expert put it, "Wall Street produced a blizzard of increasingly complex new securities," based on mortgages that these Wall Street firms had purchased.

There were data on conventional mortgages, going back for generations, including periods of inflation or deflation, war and peace, and other changing conditions. But many of the new kinds of mortgages had become a major part of the housing market within very recent years. Yet the long-established, worldwide reputation of financial rating firms like Moody's and Standard & Poor's caused many investors to rely heavily on the good ratings they gave to many of the new financial securities. Investors around the world were later caught short when some of these securities turned out to be far less reliable than their ratings would have indicated.

Another element in the housing markets were lenders who knew how to take advantage of less knowledgeable homeowners, some of whom already owned their homes outright. Unscrupulous lenders would lend, not with the goal of being repaid but with the prospect of being able to foreclose on the property of homeowners who had signed agreements they did not understand. These were called "predatory lenders." Sometimes such racketeers did repairs or remodeling on credit, at inflated prices, and with contracts that only the uninformed or unwary were likely to sign.

Such shady operators are basically a problem for the criminal justice system. Yet the concept of "predatory lenders" has become widely applied loosely to all kinds of *other* situations and institutions whose only common denominator is that critics don't like them or don't understand them. The Federal Reserve System, which collects vast amounts of data on many aspects of lending, has no definition of "predatory lending." Many in politics have acted as if predatory lenders are what caused the housing crisis— a view especially common among those who themselves had a major role in bringing on the crisis.

All these things added to the growing riskiness of housing market finances.

When it comes to the home mortgage boom and bust, who was to blame? The borrowers? The lenders? The government? The financial markets?

The answer is yes. All were responsible and many were irresponsible.

Economics cannot explain such things. For that, we must turn to the politics of housing.

Chapter 2

The Politics of the Housing Boom

The new and risky methods of financing home purchases that rose to dominance in the early years of the twenty-first century could not have replaced more traditional rules and standards for granting mortgage loans unless those who regulated banks and other lending institutions had agreed to such changes. In reality, government agencies not only approved the more lax standards for mortgage loan applicants, government officials were in fact the driving force behind the loosening of mortgage loan requirements.

Members of Congress from both political parties have urged federal regulatory agencies to press banks and other lenders to lower mortgage loan requirements, and have passed legislation to that end and to subsidize or guarantee loans made under lowered standards. Presidents of both parties, in different ways, pushed the idea that a higher rate of home ownership was "a good thing." In 1999, the *New York Times* reported:

> In a move that could help increase home ownership rates among minorities and low-income consumers, the Fannie Mae Corporation is easing the credit requirements on loans that it will purchase from banks and other lenders. . .
>
> Fannie Mae, the nation's biggest underwriter of home mortgages, has been under increasing pressure from the Clinton Administration to expand mortgage loans among low and moderate income people and felt pressure from stock holders to maintain its phenomenal growth in profits.

There were many who shared the responsibility— or, in this case, the irresponsibility— for the housing boom that was fueled by easier credit, lower mortgage approval standards and "creative" financing. Moreover, like many disasters, this one began with good intentions. At the heart of those good intentions was the quest for "affordable housing," another way of expressing the crusade for more home ownership among a wider range of people.

"AFFORDABLE HOUSING"

While the term "affordable housing" has not been defined in any absolute sense, the usual way of measuring whether housing is more affordable or less affordable in one place compared to another, or in one time period compared to another, is by comparing what percentage of an average income has to be paid for the average rent or the average monthly mortgage payment. At one time, the rule of thumb was that housing costs should not take more than one-fourth of a family's income. Others have suggested 30 percent but, whatever the number, it is meaningful only for comparing one place with another or one time period with another.

Affordability can also be measured by comparing the *total* cost— not just the monthly mortgage payments— of the average house at a given place with the average annual income of the people who live there. For example, the median home price in Youngstown, Ohio, has been found to be roughly double the median income in Youngstown. The median home price in Las Vegas has been about six times the median income in that city and, in San Diego, the median home price has been ten times the median income.

As a rough rule of thumb for making comparisons, "affordable housing" can be a useful concept. In another sense, however, the concept of "affordable housing" conceals an assumption and an agenda that are very much in need of scrutiny. Each individual knows what can and cannot be afforded on that individual's income. In other words, those who can afford mansions can buy mansions and those who can afford bungalows can buy bungalows. Those who cannot afford to buy any house can rent a house or rent an apartment, and those who cannot yet afford even that can double up with relatives or roommates, or can rent a room. Many people have done some or all of these things at one period of their lives or another.

But that is *not* what is meant by those who set up a political goal of "affordable housing." The *political* meaning of affordable housing is that individuals choose their housing and government somehow makes it financially possible for them to have it. This is seldom spelled out explicitly, much less reasoned out in terms of its implications. Much of political rhetoric serves as a substitute for reasoning.

A National Problem?

At the heart of many arguments for federal intervention in housing markets has been the belief that a shortage of affordable housing is a nationwide problem, for which local solutions are inadequate. According to a *New York Times* editorial in 2002, "the housing crisis will never be solved unless the federal government gets back into the game." *Washington Post* columnist David Broder likewise saw the problem as national in scope, that "in almost every city I've visited this year, from Sacramento to Tallahassee to Boston, the shortage of affordable housing is close to the top of people's concerns."

There is, of course, no way to know how representative either the cities that Mr. Broder visited or the people that he talked to were, much less whether their perceptions or interests corresponded to empirical reality. As J.A. Schumpeter said: "You can travel far and wide and yet wear blinkers wherever you go."

Indeed, a *New York Times* news report flatly contradicted what was said in the *New York Times* editorial just cited: "A sharp fall in mortgage rates since the early 1980's, a decline in mortgage fees and a rise in incomes have more than made up for rising house prices in almost every place outside of New York, Washington, Miami and along the coast in California." An earlier study by the Heritage Foundation likewise found that "the ratio of monthly cost-to-gross income decreased"— rather than increased— again, with the exception of "a few metropolitan markets on the East and West coasts."

Other scholarly research has likewise found that affordable housing, by common standards, has been the norm across most of the country, but with glaring exceptions in places where average housing prices are some multiple of what they are in the nation as a whole. Almost invariably, as noted in Chapter 1, these are places where severe local government restrictions on land use, and other impediments to building, have driven the cost of houses and of apartment rents to levels that take as much as half of the average family's income just to put a roof over their heads. For the country as a whole, however, home buyers have paid no more than the old-fashioned standard of 25 percent of their incomes for housing in any year since 1985. Renters have in recent years paid a somewhat higher percentage of their smaller incomes but not more than 30 percent in any year over the past several decades.

Neither by comparison with the recent past nor by comparison with other countries today is most housing in the United States unaffordable. The median-priced home in the United States as a whole is 3.6 times the median income of Americans. For Great Britain, the median-priced home is 5.5 times the median income and, in Australia and New Zealand, the ratio of home prices to income is 6.3.

Acknowledging this reality would cause a widely accepted vision, and the national crusades and policies built upon it, to collapse like a house of cards. Instead, facts that would undermine this vision and this political crusade have been largely ignored.

Despite the widespread assumption that government intervention is the key to making housing affordable to people of moderate or low incomes, history shows that it has been precisely in the times and places where government intervention has been greatest that housing costs have been both highest in absolute terms and have taken a larger share of the average income. This is true whether we compare different places at the same time or different time periods with one another. If we look back to the beginning of the twentieth century, when government played a much smaller role in the housing market and there were far fewer restrictions on building, the average American's housing costs were a *smaller* share of consumer expenditures than at the end of that century.

Back in 1901, housing costs were 23 percent of consumer expenditures. But, by 2003, housing costs were 33 percent of much higher consumer expenditures. There are local data that tell a very similar story:

> Until 1970, median homes in nearly all U.S. metropolitan areas typically cost about twice as much as median family incomes in those areas. Depending on the prevailing interest rate, this meant that a family dedicating a quarter of its income to a mortgage could pay off a loan for a home in a little more than 10 years.

Even in coastal California, home prices were very affordable *before* the severe housing restrictions that began there during the 1970s. As late as 1969, the median-priced home in San Francisco cost no more than 2.3 times the median family income in San Francisco at that time. That same year, the median price of a home in San Jose was 2.2 times the median family income in San Jose. Spending one-fourth of the median family income on monthly mortgage payments would pay off the mortgage in 12 years. A decade later, the median family home in San Jose cost 4 times the median family income in San Jose— and now it would take 40 percent of the family's income to pay off the mortgage in 30 years. By 2005, at the height of the housing boom, the median price of a home in San Jose was 7.5 times the median family income there.

These variations in the affordability of housing prices over time tell essentially the same story as variations in the affordability of housing prices from place to place at a given time: Where there is the greatest government intervention, housing is least affordable. Nor is this pattern confined to the United States. As noted in Chapter 1, in 23 of the 26 urban areas around the world where housing is rated "severely unaffordable," there are severe land use restrictions under the heading of "smart-growth" policies.

Advocates of "affordable housing" seldom— if ever— seek to remove government restrictions that have led to higher housing prices. Instead, they seek various ways of either forcing the private sector to charge lower home prices and lower apartment rents, or else they seek to use the taxpayers' money to subsidize housing in one way or another. In other words, they do not seek to reduce the government's role in the housing market but to increase it. They do not seek to *lower* housing costs but to *conceal* housing costs with taxpayer-provided subsidies or with laws that prevent those costs from being expressed in the prices charged.

Whether or not programs or policies to artificially lower housing prices or monthly mortgage payments have been enough to offset other government policies that artificially raise housing prices, both local and national government policies are among the factors which have set the stage for the housing boom and bust.

Lowering Lending Standards

In recent times, government officials have increasingly pressured banks and other lenders to lend to people whom they would not lend to otherwise. One of the first federal government efforts to change the process of mortgage lending by private financial institutions was the Community Reinvestment Act of 1977. Like many government policies or programs, it began small and grew in scope and severity over the years.

The Community Reinvestment Act directed "each appropriate Federal financial supervisory agency to use its authority when examining financial institutions, to encourage such institutions to help meet the credit needs of the local communities in which they are chartered consistent with the safe and sound operation of such institutions."

These almost innocuous words nevertheless contain the implicit assumption that government officials are qualified to tell lenders to whom they should lend money entrusted to them by depositors or investors. Yet this remarkable assumption received little scrutiny, either when the Community Reinvestment Act was passed or since.

Although the Community Reinvestment Act had no major immediate impact, over the years its underlying assumptions and provisions provided the basis for ever more insistent pressure on lenders from a variety of government officials and agencies to lend to those whom politicians and bureaucrats wanted them to lend to, rather than to those that lenders would have chosen to lend to on the basis of the lenders' own experience and expertise.

These pressures began to build in the 1990s and increased exponentially thereafter. Studies in the early 1990s, showing different mortgage loan approval rates for blacks and whites, set off media sensations and denunciations, leading to both Congressional and White House pressures on agencies regulating banks to impose new lending rules, and to monitor statistics on the loan approval rates by race, by community and by income, with penalties on banks and other lenders for failing to meet politically-imposed norms or quotas. These stepped-up pressures began during the George H.W. Bush administration and escalated during the Clinton administration, when Attorney General Janet Reno threatened legal action against lenders whose racial statistics raised her suspicions.

It would be too much of a detour at this point to go into the details of these claims of racial discrimination by mortgage lenders, but that will be done in Chapter 4. However, even at this point, the idea that lenders would be offended by receiving monthly mortgage payment checks in the mail from blacks should at least give us pause. It should also be noted that a substantial majority of both blacks and whites had their mortgage loan applications approved. The issue has been about the statistical difference between these approval rates, not any claim that most blacks could not get mortgage loans.

Although many in the media and in politics treat statistical differences in outcomes as evidence of differences in the way people are treated— in this case, racial discrimination— this assumption is inconsistent with the plain fact that (1) statistical differences among groups are both large and common, in countries around the world, even in situations where these differences cannot be explained by discrimination,* and (2) lenders are in business to make money. Yet even people who are quick to denounce corporate "greed" often also argue inconsistently as if lenders are arbitrarily withholding their favors from people they don't like. Lenders are not doing favors by making loans, any more than Campbell's is doing favors by selling soup. Lenders would be cutting their own throats financially if they arbitrarily denied loans to people with good prospects of paying them back with interest.

Whatever the merits, or lack of merits, of the logic or evidence on which charges of biased lending were based, the political impact of such beliefs has been powerful. Moreover, even though racial bias charges provided much of the initial impetus for greater federal government involvement in private mortgage lending decisions, once federal regulatory agencies became involved that involvement spread far beyond issues of race, and the policies imposed required a lowering of mortgage loan approval standards across the board, to people of all races.

It is by no means clear that minority mortgage loan applicants were the main beneficiaries— or that they necessarily benefitted at all, on net balance, when their loan default rates and home foreclosure rates were especially high

---

*For dozens of examples from countries around the world, just in books of mine, see *The Vision of the Anointed*, pp. 35–37; *Conquests and Cultures*, p. 125; *Migrations and Cultures*, pp. 4, 17, 30, 31, 56–57, 118, 121, 122–123, 126, 130, 135, 152, 154, 158, 167, 176, 179, 196, 211, 212, 224, 251, 258, 264, 265, 275, 277, 278, 289, 290, 298, 300, 305, 306, 318, 320, 324, 345–346, 353–356, 358, 366, 373.

during the later housing bust. In any event, the *application* of the principles of the Community Reinvestment act evolved in practice:

> In 1995, the regulators created new rules that sought to establish objective criteria for determining whether a bank was meeting CRA standards. Examiners no longer had the discretion they once had. For banks, simply proving that they were looking for qualified buyers wasn't enough. Banks now had to show that they had actually made a requisite number of loans to low- and moderate-income (LMI) borrowers. The new regulations also required the use of "innovative or flexible" lending practices to address credit needs of LMI borrowers and neighborhoods.

In plain English, the regulators imposed quotas— and, if lenders had to resort to "innovative or flexible" standards and methods to meet those quotas, so be it.

Because banks are federally regulated enterprises, they need government permission to do many things that other businesses do as they see fit. That permission can be delayed or denied when objections are made that banks or other lenders are not living up to their obligations under the Community Reinvestment Act. For example, when legislation was pending in 1999 to permit banks to diversify into selling investment securities, the White House urged "that banks given unsatisfactory ratings under the 1977 Community Reinvestment Act be prohibited from enjoying the new diversification privileges" of this legislation.

Accordingly, when Congress passed legislation removing existing prohibitions against banks affiliating with securities or insurance firms, this new scope of banking operations was in fact reserved for those banks with a "rating of 'satisfactory record of meeting community credit needs', or better, at the most recent examination of each such institution"— that is, banks that met government-imposed quotas.

These were not the only government pressures on banks to fulfill lending quotas. In 1993, the Department of Housing and Urban Development "began bringing legal actions against mortgage bankers that declined a higher percentage of minority applicants than white applicants." Lenders then began lowering their down payment requirements and income requirements. HUD also brought pressures to bear on Fannie Mae and Freddie Mac to increase their purchases of mortgages made to low-income and moderate-income home buyers. In 1996 HUD set a target that 42 percent of the mortgages bought by Fannie Mae and Freddie Mac were to be financed for people with incomes below the median income in their areas.

Various community activists across the country have been able to pressure banks into making concessions in money or in kind, in order to get those activists to withdraw their objections to pending bank mergers or to banks opening new branches in another state, for example. The *Wall Street Journal* reported:

> Increasingly, community activists are taking banks to task—and winning large financial concessions— under the federal Community Reinvestment Act. . . This year alone, banks are expected to pony up $1 billion in low-cost loans and other aid for such causes as housing for the poor and the development of inner-city businesses. Wells Fargo Bank is providing low-cost financing for a shelter for battered women. First National Bank of Chicago is helping finance work on the headquarters of the National Training and Information Center, a major community-action group.

As regulatory agencies began to require reports on banks' "community service" activities under the Community Reinvestment Act before granting permission for mergers or opening branch offices, banks began to expand such things as donations to local non-profit agencies, establishing quotas for hiring of bank employees and set aside a certain amount of business for firms owned by ethnic minorities. Sumitomo Bank of California, for example, declared that it would give 20 to 25 percent of its contracts to minority-owned businesses.

Despite the title of the Community Reinvestment Act, it was not just in particular communities that lenders were pressured to make loans that they would not have made otherwise. Banks' qualification standards for lending to individuals in general were also attacked as too stringent as regards down payments, income, credit histories and other standards. In the housing markets, lenders were increasingly pressured by federal officials to relax lending standards, so as to make mortgage loans to people whose incomes and credit histories would not make them eligible under the traditional standards.

Not only did banks and other direct mortgage lenders respond to these pressures, so did the giant government-sponsored enterprises Fannie Mae and Freddie Mac, by lowering their standards for the kinds of mortgages that they would purchase from the banks and other direct mortgage lenders. The *New York Times* reported:

> "Fannie Mae has expanded home ownership for millions of families in the 1990's by reducing down payment requirements," said Franklin D. Raines, Fannie Mae's chairman and chief executive officer. "Yet there remain too many borrowers whose credit is just a notch below what our underwriting has required who have been relegated to paying significantly higher mortgage rates in the so-called subprime market."

This statement clearly pointed toward lowering other requirements— and that is in fact what happened.

In 2002, the George W. Bush administration urged Congress to pass the American Dream Downpayment Act, which subsidized the down payments of prospective home buyers whose incomes were below a certain level. After passage of that Act, the president also urged Congress to pass legislation permitting the Federal Housing Administration to begin making zero-down-payment loans at low interest rates to low-income Americans. In 2004, Federal Housing Commissioner John Weicher said, "the White House doesn't think those who can afford the monthly payment but have been unable to save for a down payment should be deprived from owning a home." He added, "We do not anticipate any costs to taxpayers." Who, if not the taxpayers, would pay for these government subsidies— much less the defaults from making riskier loans— was not revealed.

For some home buyers, the standards were relaxed to the point where there was no down payment at all required, contrary to a long-standing tradition that home buyers should have some stake in the home, so as to reduce the risk of default on the mortgage. The reduction or elimination of traditional safeguards in mortgage lending entailed a rising riskiness of the mortgages acquired by Fannie Mae and Freddie Mac under the new and lower mortgage loan approval standards.

Under these political pressures, traditional mortgage loans with traditional safeguards began to decline and mortgage loans made under the "innovative" and "flexible" standards urged by government increased. Traditional 30-year mortgages with a fixed interest rate, which were still 57 percent of all mortgages in 2001, fell to 33 percent of all mortgages by the end of 2006. Meanwhile, subprime loans rose from 7 percent of all mortgage loans to become 19 percent of such loans over the same span of years. Other non-traditional loans rose from less than 3 percent of all mortgage loans to nearly 14 percent.

Between 2005 and 2007, Fannie Mae and Freddie Mac acquired an estimated trillion dollars' worth of subprime and other non-traditional mortgages. This was approximately 40 percent of the value of all the mortgages they purchased from banks and other lenders during those years. In other words, these two major institutions of the mortgage markets were acquiring increasingly risky assets.

What was crucial was that the Department of Housing and Urban Development, which was among the federal agencies pushing Fannie Mae and Freddie Mac to make more loans to people who would not normally be approved for loans— the "underserved" population, in the phrase often used— "allowed Freddie Mac and Fannie Mae to count billions of dollars they invested in subprime loans as a public good that would foster affordable housing," according to the *Washington Post*.

In short, riskier loans were accepted as good loans by one of the key regulators of the housing markets. Moreover, HUD was not just accepting subprime lending but pushing for more. After HUD became a regulator of Fannie Mae and Freddie Mac in 1992, these government-sponsored enterprises were set numerical goals— quotas— for what share of their lending was to be for "affordable housing" mortgages. In practice, they were pushed to acquire more subprime mortgages.

This was important not only because of the risk to the assets of these two enterprises themselves but, because they are dominant forces in the housing market and major gigantic financial institutions, there were dangers to the whole financial market if things went wrong with Fannie Mae and Freddie Mac, whose securities were widely held by other financial institutions in Wall Street and beyond. The importance of Fannie Mae and Freddie Mac in the housing markets is demonstrated by the magnitude of their mortgage guarantees, which total more than two *trillion* dollars. That is larger than the Gross Domestic Product of all but four nations.

Ordinarily, financial markets would become less willing to invest in an enterprise with ever growing risks. But, although Fannie Mae and Freddie Mac are officially private, profit-making enterprises, their size and the federal government's involvement in both their creation and their on-going operations led many investors to assume that the federal government would never allow them to fail— which is to say, the increasing riskiness of the assets of these two mortgage market giants was an increasing riskiness for the taxpayers, whether the taxpayers knew it or not. Moreover, "creative" accounting *within* Fannie Mae and Freddie Mac themselves concealed the full extent of the risk until independent audits turned up discrepancies at both places, which led to the resignation of the heads of both institutions.

In short, the policies and practices of many institutions, local and national, public and private, set the stage for the housing boom and the housing bust that followed. Placing the roots of the housing boom and bust in the market and the solution in government is very convenient for politicians and for those who favor government interventions. But such explanations are inconsistent with facts, however impressive they might be as exercises in rhetoric.

Both the genesis of unaffordable housing in particular local areas and the responses with national policies to make buying a home easier were political in origin, and government regulation is what forced lenders to meet arbitrary quotas by eroding traditional mortgage lending safeguards. The facts could not be plainer. Market criteria had long required such things as substantial down payments, as well as income and credit histories that made continuing payments likely. But all that was brushed aside in the political crusade for "affordable housing" and bigger home ownership statistics.

Both the unrealistic nature of policies pursued in the name of "affordable housing" and the serious dangers that such policies posed to the entire economy provoked many warnings from economists and others. But these warnings were repeatedly brushed aside by political leaders, often by shifting the focus to the supposed benefits of creating more home ownership through "affordable housing."

WARNINGS

Many people (including the author of this book) pointed out some of the problems and risks during the housing boom. As far away as London, the distinguished British magazine *The Economist* in 2003 reiterated a warning it had made before, that "house prices would fall by 10% in America over the next four years," though it acknowledged that many of its readers "reject our gloomy warnings." In reality, American house prices fell sooner and more steeply. By 2005, *The Economist* repeated their warning yet again, but more urgently: "America's house prices have reached dangerous levels" and added: "The whole world economy is at risk."

In 2003, U.S. Secretary of the Treasury John W. Snow asked Congress to "enact legislation to create a new Federal agency to regulate and supervise" Fannie Mae and Freddie Mac, because of his concerns about the risks they were taking. Two years later, testifying before the same Congressional committee, he returned to the same theme, citing the "systemic risk" arising from the fact that securities issued by Fannie Mae and Freddie Mac were "out there in the marketplace, held by all sorts of financial institutions—insurance companies, pension plans, community banks, thrifts, commercial banks." He added: "The concern is, if something unravels, it could cause systemic risk to the whole financial system." In 2003, *Newsweek* economist Robert J. Samuelson pointed out that about 3,000 banks held Fannie Mae and Freddie Mac "debt equal to all their capital."

In 2004, Josh Rosner, an analyst at Medley Global Advisors in New York, said, "The move to push home-ownership on people that historically would not have had the finances or credit to qualify could conceivably and ultimately turn Fannie Mae's American dream of homeownership into the American nightmare of homeownership where people are trapped in their homes." He added: "If incomes don't rise or home values don't keep rising, or if interest rates rose considerably, you could quickly end up with significantly more people underwater with their mortgages and unable to pay."

A 2004 article in *Fortune* magazine also warned of housing speculation that "is rapidly losing touch with reality" and of the risks created by the growing practice of borrowing against the equity in one's home. It warned that "there's a real danger that a downturn in prices, or even a stall, could slam the economy, especially all-important consumer spending. Americans have used their homes like ATMs, taking out $662 billion in home-equity loans and refinancings since 2001."

In 2005, resident scholar Peter J. Wallison of the American Enterprise Institute, a Washington think tank, warned that, if Congress did not rein in Fannie Mae and Freddie Mac, "there will be a massive default with huge losses to the taxpayers and systemic effects on the economy."

Although most of the strongest supporters of lowering mortgage approval standards were Democrats, President George W. Bush joined in the political push for more home ownership, drawing the criticism of *Barron's* magazine:

One of the proudest elements of President Bush's "compassionate conservative" agenda has been government financial support to home buyers for down payments. . . . But he is exposing taxpayers to tens of billions of dollars of possible losses, luring thousands of moderate-income families into bankruptcy, and risking the destruction of entire neighborhoods. . . . Free down payments carry catastrophic risks. . . Transferring the risk of homeownership from buyers to taxpayers does not endow virtue in America. Giving people a handout that leads them to financial ruin is wrecking-ball benevolence.

The head of the Federal Deposit Insurance Corporation warned Congress about "increasing numbers of problem loans, and concentrations of higher risk loans as a percentage of capital."

Federal Reserve Chairman Alan Greenspan was the best-known public figure to issue warnings on the housing boom. His warnings, like those of the Secretary of the Treasury and the head of the Federal Deposit Insurance Corporation, were delivered directly to Congress, while testifying there. Alan Greenspan over the years moved from expressions of mild concern to a more dire view of the situation.

In 2005, Chairman Greenspan testified: "Although a bubbling in home prices for the Nation as a whole does not appear likely, there do appear to be at a minimum signs of froth in some local markets where home prices seem to have risen to unsustainable levels." Greenspan did note "the prevalence of interest-only loans, as well as the introduction of other relatively exotic forms of adjustable rate mortgages" as "developments of particular concern." But he added: "Although we certainly cannot rule out home price declines, especially in some local markets, these declines, were they to occur, likely would not have substantial macro-economic implications."

Although Chairman Greenspan at this point seemed not to expect major problems from the housing booms in various localities around the country, he was already apprehensive about the longer-run consequences of the expansion of Fannie Mae and Freddie Mac. He said, "if they continue to grow, continue to have the low capital that they have," then "they potentially create ever growing potential systemic risks down the road." There was, in his judgment, "no risk now at the moment," so there was time "to do something to fend off problems, which in my judgment seem almost inevitable as we look forward into the remainder of this decade." He opposed "enabling these institutions to increase in size," and added:

> We are placing the total financial system of the future at a substantial risk. Fortunately, at this stage, the risk is, the best I can judge, virtually negligible. I don't believe that will be the case if we continue to expand in this system.

By 2007, however, after Alan Greenspan was no longer chairman of the Federal Reserve System, and after housing prices had begun to fall, his concerns were heightened. He told the *Financial Times* of London that turmoil in the financial markets was "an accident waiting to happen." In a television interview on *60 Minutes*, Greenspan admitted that he had not fully assessed the extent of the dangers from the new ways of financing home mortgages. "While I was aware a lot of these practices were going on, I had no notion of how significant they had become until very late," he said. "I really didn't get it until very late in 2005 and 2006."

Many in Congress and elsewhere never really got it.

In response to warnings about the growing riskiness in housing markets, Congressman Barney Frank said in 2003, "Fannie Mae and Freddie Mac have played a very useful role in helping make housing more affordable." Critics "exaggerate a threat of safety" and "conjure up the possibility of serious financial losses to the Treasury, which I do not see."

As for government pressures on Fannie Mae and Freddie Mac to loosen their mortgage lending standards, he said: "I believe that we, as the Federal Government, have probably done too little rather than too much to push them to meet the goals of affordable housing and to set reasonable goals." He said, "I would like to get Fannie and Freddie more deeply into helping low-income housing and possibly moving into something that is more explicitly a subsidy." He added: "I want to roll the dice a little bit more in this situation towards subsidized housing."

Congressman Frank expressed a fear that criticisms of lower lending standards could create pressures to tighten those standards, because "the more pressure there is there, then the less I think we see in terms of affordable housing."

Congressman Frank dismissed fears expressed by those who saw an implicit commitment by the federal government to bail out Fannie Mae and Freddie Mac that could lead these giants to engage in more risky financial operations, because they felt they were backed up by the government, and this could lead investors to go along with accepting their risky securities, based on the same implicit reliance on the federal treasury. "But there is no guarantee," Congressman Frank asserted, "there is no explicit guarantee, there is no implicit guarantee, there is no wink-and-nod guarantee."

Such statements were not just some popping off by an isolated politician. Barney Frank was in 2003 the ranking member of the House Committee on Financial Services and would later become chairman of that powerful committee in 2006. He was a very influential force in the housing market.

Later events, however, were not kind to Congressman Frank's assertions. Those investors who had relied on taxpayer bailouts of Fannie Mae and Freddie Mac turned out to be right and Barney Frank wrong. As of January 2009, Fannie Mae and Freddie Mac were in line to receive

$238 billion in federal bailout money and were asking for $70 billion more.

Congressman Frank was by no means the only member of Congress to dismiss warnings and assert that Fannie Mae and Freddie Mac were safe and sound institutions. His counterpart in the Senate, Chairman Christopher Dodd of the Senate Banking Committee, was equally adamant on the subject and continued to be so equally long— well into 2008, long after the financial system had already gone into a historic collapse. Back in 2004, when Fannie Mae and Freddie Mac were under criticism, Senator Dodd called them "one of the great success stories of all time" and urged "caution" in restricting their activities, out of fear of "doing great damage to what has been one of the great engines of economic success in the last 30 or 40 years."

After accounting errors totaling $11 billion were discovered in the books of Fannie Mae and Freddie Mac, President Bush in 2007 said that these government-sponsored enterprises should complete "a robust reform package" before being allowed to expand their mortgage portfolios. Senator Dodd said that President Bush should "immediately reconsider his ill-advised" position. As late as July 2008, after the housing market had collapsed, Senator Dodd continued to defend Fannie Mae and Freddie Mac as being "on a sound footing." Later events did not deal kindly with this assertion, as both these hybrid enterprises were bailed out to prevent their collapse and were taken over by the federal government.

Over the years, both houses of Congress had many defenders of Fannie Mae and Freddie Mac as promoters of the political crusade for "affordable housing" through lower mortgage lending standards. Congresswoman Maxine Waters said in 2003, "we do not have a crisis at Freddie Mac, and in particular at Fannie Mae, under the outstanding leadership of Mr. Frank Raines." (This was the same Franklin Raines who would later resign after the accounting scandals at Fannie Mae came to light.) Maxine Waters added that any regulatory reforms "must be done in a manner so as not to impede their affordable housing mission, a mission that has seen innovation flourish from desktop underwriting to 100 percent loans."

It was precisely these "desktop loans" based on unsubstantiated income claims by applicants— "liar loans" critics called them— and loans with no down payment at all ("100 percent loans") that many saw as especially dangerous.

Congressman Joe Baca likewise made "affordable housing" his over-riding concern. "According to Fannie Mae's own research," he said, with each rise of a quarter of a percent in the interest rate "some 78,166 Hispanic and 107,158 African American families become unable to afford to purchase a home." Moreover, "a long protracted debate on regulation" could cause "instability of the markets." In other words, just talking about the risks and the need for regulation could reduce the over-riding goal of more home ownership through "affordable housing." Such statements are reminiscent of Admiral Farragut's famous battle cry, "Damn the torpedoes, full speed ahead!" In this case, however, the financial markets got torpedoed and the whole economy sank.

In June 2004, in response to President Bush's expressed concerns about the riskiness of Fannie Mae and Freddie Mac, seventy-six Democrats in the House of Representatives sent him a letter defending these government-sponsored enterprises, and again making the case that "an exclusive focus on safety and soundness is likely to come, in practice, at the expense of affordable housing." These 76 House members included such prominent individuals as Nancy Pelosi, Barney Frank, Maxine Waters and Charles Rangel.

Not only members of Congress, but others with a vested interest in lower mortgage lending standards, staunchly defended those standards in general and Fannie Mae and Freddie Mac in particular, during the housing boom that others were warning about. People in the business of building homes obviously have a vested interest in government policies and programs that cause more homes to be built. Therefore it should not be surprising that a representative of the National Association of Homebuilders testified before the House Committee on Financial Services in favor of existing low standards for mortgage loan approval:

> In focusing on safety and soundness regulation, we urge the committee not to lose sight of the core missions, which is. . .to provide liquidity, capital and stability to the housing market. . .
>
> The objective and focus of program oversight is not safety and soundness, as HUD Secretary Martinez testified, it is mission compliance. An example would be furthering the Administration's goal of increasing minority home ownership.

In other words, so long as more homes got built, the National Association of Homebuilders was not going to sweat the details, which would ultimately be the taxpayers' problem. The National Urban League likewise saw the whole issue in terms of its own constituency. An official of the Urban League testified before the same committee that any oversight of Fannie Mae and Freddie Mac should "fit into a coherent set of programs at HUD to create the largest affordable housing stock available for America, and that huge disparities in home ownership faced by African-Americans and Hispanics can be closed."

The heads of Fannie Mae and Freddie Mac also went on record in favor of mortgage lending standards that focused on "affordable housing" more so than on financial standards. The Director of Freddie Mac, after gingerly referring in passing to "the resolution of Freddie Mac's accounting issues," went on to say that "we have consistently met the permanent affordable housing goals" and that "Freddie Mac is safe, sound and strong."

The CEO of Fannie Mae, the already mentioned Franklin Raines, likewise said that every year "we have met or exceeded our affordable housing goals, even as they have increased" and that Fannie Mae has "also set a voluntary goal: to lead the market in serving minority families." Moreover, CEO Raines pointed out in passing that Fannie Mae had "amassed over $30 billion of private equity capital to finance $2 trillion of mortgages today." He did not address the critics' charge that it was precisely this very high ratio of business done to the amount of capital available, to cover any problems that might arise, which posed a major risk to Fannie Mae and to the financial system in general, which held such vast amounts of Fannie Mae's securities.

Congressional support for Fannie Mae and Freddie Mac went far beyond words. When the Office of Federal Housing Enterprise Oversight— the agency overseeing these government-sponsored enterprises— turned up irregularities in Fannie Mae's accounting and in 2004 issued what *Barron's* magazine called "a blistering 211-page report," Republican Senator Kit Bond called for an investigation *of the Office of Federal Housing Enterprise Oversight*, tried to have their budget slashed, and sought to have the leadership of the regulatory agency removed. Democratic Congressman Barney Frank likewise declared: "It is clear that a leadership change at OFHEO is overdue."

In short, Fannie Mae's political support in Congress has been bipartisan. "Fannie Mae and Freddie Mac's employees and political action committees donated nearly $5 million to current members of Congress since 1989," according to the *St. Louis Post-Dispatch*. Senator Kit Bond received $95,000 and Senator Christopher Dodd received $165,000. According to the *Wall Street Journal*:

> The two companies employ armies of lobbyists and consultants and are major campaign donors. "There has been no more powerful organization in Washington than Fannie Mae," said Rep. Chris Shays (R., Conn.). "They have been able to manipulate the regulatory and legislative process for years."

Such criticisms of the political protection of Fannie Mae and Freddie Mac were not confined to conservative publications like the *Wall Street Journal*. Essentially the same criticisms were made in the liberal *Washington Post*:

> Blessed with the advantages of a government agency and a private company at the same time, Fannie Mae and Freddie Mac used their windfall profits to co-opt the politicians who were supposed to control them. The companies fought successfully against increased regulation by cultivating their friends and hounding their enemies. . . . The agencies that regulated the companies were outmatched: They lacked the money, the staff, the sophistication and the political support to serve as an effective check.

This pattern went back for years. The *Washington Post* recalled a 1992 attempt by Congressman Jim Leach to get stronger regulation of Fannie Mae and Freddie Mac— and the opposition by Congressman Barney Frank to prevent it. The *Washington Post* also pointed out how the budget of the Office of Federal Housing Enterprise Oversight, which regulated Fannie Mae and Freddie Mac, was more tightly controlled by Congress than were the budgets of agencies regulating banks, giving the two hybrid companies' "congressional allies an easy way to exert pressure" on OFHEO and limit its ability to regulate. Moreover, the rules on capital requirements for Fannie Mae and Freddie Mac were less strict than the rules for banks, allowing these government-sponsored enterprises greater opportunities for profit.

Corruption of the political process can take many forms. Senator Christopher Dodd, for example, received mortgages from Countrywide Financial Corporation on unusually favorable terms, saving him an estimated $75,000. Senator Bob Bennett of Utah not only received more campaign contributions from Fannie Mae and Freddie Mac than any other Republican in Congress over the years, his son was employed by Fannie Mae. *The Economist* magazine reported: "Ex-politicians were given jobs" by Fannie Mae and Freddie Mac.

One of the other perquisites of power has long been simply the ability to throw one's weight around. Although the Massachusetts-based bank called OneUnited was ineligible to receive money from the Troubled Asset Relief Program (TARP) under its general guidelines, Massachusetts Congressman Barney Frank intervened and suddenly it became eligible to receive $12 million of the taxpayers' money. According to the *Wall Street Journal*, "Mr. Frank, by his own account, wrote into the TARP bill a provision specifically aimed at helping this particular home-state bank. And later, he acknowledges, he spoke to regulators urging that OneUnited be considered for a cash injection." At a meeting with U.S. Treasury Department officials were not only representatives of Congressman Barney Frank but also representatives of Senator John Kerry of Massachusetts and of Congresswoman Maxine Waters of Los Angeles, whose husband had served on the board of directors of the OneUnited Bank and has had at least a quarter of a million dollars worth of stock in the bank.

Fear, as well as favors, help explain how some programs and institutions become sacred cows. According to economist Gerald P. O'Driscoll, a former official of the Federal Reserve System and a former executive in private banking, before becoming a scholar in residence at the Cato Institute:

> At heart, Fannie and Freddie had become classic examples of "crony capitalism." The "cronies" were businessmen and politicians working together to line each other's pockets while claiming to serve the public good. The politicians created the mortgage giants, which then returned some of the profits to the pols— sometimes directly, as campaign funds; sometimes as "contributions" to favored constituents. . . .And, because government backing let Fannie and Freddie dominate the mortgage-underwriting market, private-sector criticism was silenced. Local banks that wanted to offer mortgages dared not speak out against them. Large banks dared not complain about the giants' government-given advantage because they needed to be able to buy securities from Fannie/Freddie.

Chapter 3

The Housing Bust

Back in 2002, *Newsweek* economic columnist Robert J. Samuelson wrote:

> To anyone with a sense of history, the home boom must be a source of wonder. Housing usually leads the economy into recession. Mortgage rates rise, then housing construction and home sales fall.

This historical pattern repeated yet again, just four years later. The "blame game" of finger-pointing began immediately, many in politics and the media saying that the problem was that the market was left unregulated and now the government had to step in.

The development of lax lending standards, both by banks and by Fannie Mae and Freddie Mac standing behind the banks, came *not* from a lack of government regulation and oversight, but precisely as a *result* of government regulation and oversight, directed toward the politically popular goal of more "home ownership" through "affordable housing," especially for low-income home buyers. These lax lending standards were the foundation for a house of cards that was ready to collapse with a relatively small nudge.

That nudge came as the Federal Reserve System, having lowered its own interest rates to an extremely low one percent, began slowly raising the interest rate back toward more normal levels in 2004. Unusually low interest rates had been used earlier by the Federal Reserve, in order to maintain credit spending in the economy at large, at a time when the economy seemed about to decline otherwise. But such extremely low interest rates could not be maintained indefinitely, without an unending supply of easy credit leading to inflation. Federal Reserve authorities therefore began gradually but steadily raising their interest rate over time, from its low of one percent in 2004 until the Federal Reserve's interest rate reached 5.25 percent in 2006.

As financial institutions had to pay more to get money, they of course began raising their own interest rates charged to borrowers— including those borrowing to buy homes. Just as mortgage interest rates had followed Federal Reserve interest rates down, now mortgage interest rates rose as Federal Reserve interest rates rose. Then, just as unusually low interest rates had made monthly mortgage payments more affordable for more people, increasing the demand for houses and therefore their prices, conversely the rise of interest rates to more normal levels made monthly mortgage payments more expensive, and thereby reduced the demand for houses.

DECLINING HOME PRICES

Housing prices began falling in 2006, for the first time in more than a decade— and they fell by record amounts. They fell especially sharply in places where they had risen especially sharply before, which was where more people had gone farthest out on a limb with risky "creative" financing, in order to be able to buy a house, and so were most likely to default when rising interest rates meant rising monthly mortgage payments. Speculators caught owing money on mortgages on multiple houses that could no longer be sold for rising prices— or even for the prices at which the speculators bought them— were also especially likely to default, even if that meant going bankrupt. As lenders repossessed more houses and put them up for sale, this increase in the number of houses for sale further lowered the prices of houses in general through supply and demand.

As housing prices declined in September 2006, California led the nation in mortgage foreclosures. The number of foreclosures in San Francisco and in adjoining San Mateo County were double what they had been a year earlier, and foreclosures in Alameda County across the Bay from San Francisco more than tripled in just one year.

These were not one-time events, but a continuing trend in the following years. In June 2007, foreclosure notices nationwide rose 87 percent over the previous year. In the San Francisco Bay Area, foreclosures continued to increase, nearly tripling in one year. For California as a whole, there was an 800 percent increase in the number of homes whose deeds reverted to bank ownership. This was a major problem for the banks, as well as for those who lost their homes, since banks lose an estimated $40,000 per home foreclosed. Not being in the business of managing real estate, banks have every incentive to dump repossessed houses on the market at whatever price they can get for them.

Large-scale foreclosures meant falling home prices, as the foreclosed homes added to the supply without any corresponding increase in demand. "Fully half of all existing homes sold in the Bay Area in December [2008] were foreclosures unloaded by banks at fire-sale prices," the *San Francisco Chronicle* reported. Those sales sent housing prices "tumbling to new lows and attracted droves of buyers." For the nine-county Bay Area, prices were "down 46.8 percent from a year ago," the *San Francisco Chronicle* reported. Those places outside California that had had similar sky-high prices went through a similar experience when the housing bubble burst.

Phoenix, Arizona, was described in the *New York Times* as "an epicenter of the nation's recent building boom" but that changed drastically when the housing bubble burst in 2006:

> Until recently, this fast-growing area was a paradise on earth for home builders. Fulton Homes' developments, for example, were so popular last year that it was able to raise prices on its new homes by $1,000 to $10,000 almost every week.
>
> "People were standing in line for lotteries," recalled Douglas S. Fulton, president of the company, one of the largest private builders in the Phoenix area. And they were "camping overnight begging to be the next number in the next lot in the next house."
>
> No more.
>
> Today, it is the company's sales agents that do most of the waiting. Not only are there few new customers to talk to, but many buyers who put down a deposit are not even bothering to come back for the walk-through.
>
> "All of a sudden, they just don't show up," Mr. Fulton said, noting that such cancellations often mean the buyers forfeit as much as 5 percent of the price. The reason? The prospective buyers got cold feet or simply could not sell their old home.

Sharp declines in housing prices still continued in 2008. At the end of that year, Standard & Poor's reported that its home-price index for October, compared to October of the previous year, declined more sharply than at any time in the two decades' history of that index. In October 2008, six metropolitan areas showed housing price declines of more than 25 percent, compared to the previous October, and three— Phoenix, Las Vegas and San Francisco— had housing price declines of more than 30 percent compared to October of the previous year.

Coastal California was especially hard hit. In just one year, home prices fell by 27 percent in San Diego, 28 percent in Los Angeles and 31 percent in San Francisco. A few other places had similar declines in just one year— 29 percent in

Miami, 32 percent in Las Vegas and 33 percent in Phoenix. But, of the 25 metropolitan areas with the steepest home price declines, 16 were in California. For California as a whole, home prices dropped by an average of $100,000 between 2007 and 2008. San Diego, where housing prices had more than doubled between 2000 and 2005, saw its average home price decline by more than $200,000 from 2006 to 2008.

Differential Impacts

The very different conditions in different local housing markets was demonstrated by the fact that, despite drastic declines in home prices in some areas, the nationwide housing price decline was somewhere between 2 percent and 9 percent in 2007, depending on what index was used. The home price decline was 5 percent or less in more than 50 of the metropolitan areas in the country. In fewer than 10 of the metropolitan areas had home prices declined by more than 20 percent. Meanwhile, in more than 20 metropolitan areas, home prices were still rising. Neither the sharp rise in home prices to unaffordable levels nor the subsequent fall was a nationwide phenomenon. Both were severe problems in particular localities.

In Dallas the home price decline was only 3 percent. This was in a city with few building restrictions, where housing prices took just 13 percent of the average income, even during the boom. Where housing can be had for 13 percent of the average income, there is far less incentive to go out on a limb with risky financing to buy a home— and therefore far less risk of a boom and bust in the housing market. There is also far less incentive for speculation in such a housing market. As Alan Greenspan had said back in 2005,

"We don't perceive that there is a national bubble, but it's hard not to see that there are a lot of local bubbles."

There was also a differential impact of rising interest rates on people with different kinds of mortgages. While interest rate changes did not affect existing home buyers who already had fixed-rate mortgages, these rising rates very much affected both new prospective home buyers and existing home buyers with adjustable rate mortgages, as the rise of interest rates meant increases in their monthly mortgage payments. One group particularly hard hit by the housing downturn were borrowers who used what were called "option ARMS"— adjustable rate mortgages (ARMs) with an option to vary the monthly payments at the borrower's discretion. In January 2009, the *Wall Street Journal* reported, "with home prices falling, more than 55% of borrowers with option ARMs owe more than their homes are valued at, according to J.P. Morgan Securities Inc." Twenty-eight percent of such borrowers were either delinquent or in foreclosure.

Although monthly mortgage payments by existing home buyers with the old-fashioned, fixed-rate mortgages were of course not directly affected by the rising interest rates, the value of their houses declined with that of all the rest. However, traditional fixed-rate 30-year mortgages were no longer standard but were now only about one-third of all mortgages.

Many people who had stretched to buy homes with interest-only, adjustable-rate mortgages now often found themselves pushed over the edge financially when their monthly mortgage payment rose because of rising interest rates, even before the interest-only period expired. Such borrowers were doubly affected if interest rates rose at the same time as the already scheduled monthly payment increase needed to begin paying off the principal on their mortgage loan. By 2007, about one-fourth of all adjustable-rate mortgage loans, interest-only loans and payment-option loans were at least 60 days late on their mortgage payments. This was more than double the rate of payment delinquencies on conventional 30-year fixed-rate mortgages.

The special vulnerability of borrowers with adjustable rate loans, as compared to 30-year fixed interest-rate mortgages, was reflected in the default rates and foreclosure rates during the housing downturn. In 2007, Federal Reserve Board Chairman Ben Bernanke announced: "About 320,000 foreclosures were initiated in each of the first two quarters of this year, just more than half of them on subprime mortgages, up from an average of about 220,000 during the past 6 years." According to the *New York Times*: "Minority homeowners take out a disproportionate share of subprime loans. The most recent Home Mortgage Disclosure Act data from lending institutions show that over half of African-Americans and 40 percent of Hispanics received subprime loans." Both groups were especially hard hit by the foreclosures that followed the housing bust. So much for the favor being done to minorities.

Speculators, who could make remarkable sums of money in a remarkably short amount of time during the housing boom, by borrowing at low "teaser" rates of interest and then selling quickly before these below-market rates of interest moved up to market rates, now found themselves stuck with having to pay for multiple mortgages on expensive houses that took longer to sell and could no longer be sold for more than they cost— or even for as much as they had cost. Not all of those trapped by the housing bust were innocent homeowners. Substantial numbers were people who had profited handsomely from the boom and who now wanted to be rescued from the bust with the taxpayers' money.

Research by the *San Francisco Chronicle* in 2007 turned up nearly a thousand homes in foreclosure in the San Francisco Bay Area that were "owned by 439 people who had multiple properties foreclosed upon from January to September." In addition, "349 foreclosures were owned by people who listed mailing ZIP codes different from their property's address at the time of purchase— suggesting the properties were an investment, not a primary residence." The *Las Vegas Sun* "found that 74 percent of single-family homes in foreclosure during a six-month period this year were owned by investors who did not live there." Like other aspects of the housing markets, foreclosures on property owned by absentee owners were "much more common among defaults in California, Nevada, Arizona and Florida— all states with particularly rapid price appreciation that attracted speculators."

Financial Market Repercussions

While, in a sense, the worst of the housing market collapse was geographically concentrated in places with the highest and previously fastest growing housing prices, the repercussions were nationwide and even international. Holman Jenkins of the *Wall Street Journal* called attention to "the striking fact" that much of the subprime crisis originated in particular counties in just four states.

These *locally* high housing prices, and then locally sharp declines in housing prices, in such places as coastal California, Miami or Phoenix, which had led to especially high rates of mortgage defaults, had national repercussions, because the inflated values of houses in these places were accepted by *national* organizations like Fannie Mae and Freddie Mac, which bought these mortgages, and by Wall Street firms that also bought such mortgages and then created and sold securities based on the inflated values of these mortgages across the country and overseas. Securities issued by Fannie Mae and Freddie Mac were likewise bought by both American and foreign investors. That is why a bank in Germany had to be bailed out when American housing prices fell.

As a scholarly study noted, "many of those who either sold or bought these securities were highly-sophisticated investors such as Bear Stearns, Merrill Lynch, or Citibank." But their sophistication did not save them:

> Nonetheless, numerous Wall Street titans have taken multi-billion dollar write-downs as a result of investing in securities backed by subprime loans. . . In fact, significant losses have been suffered at virtually every level of the subprime chain. . .

Part of the problem was that the era of widespread use of subprime mortgages was new, so that neither the Wall Street firms that bought them nor the credit rating firms, like Moody's or Standard & Poor's, on whose ratings the Wall Street investors relied when buying mortgage-backed securities, had much history to draw on in assessing the risks of these kinds of securities. As a study at the National Bureau of Economic Research put it, before 2006 "there was no liquid, publicly visible, market where subprime risk was directly priced. Individual transactions were priced, but these prices were not widely seen. Only the direct participants saw the prices." *The Economist* magazine called the purchase of some of these securities "a leap in the dark."

How suddenly subprime mortgages had become a major part of the financial scene was shown by the dollar volume of their growth. The value of subprime mortgages created in 1995 was $65 billion but this swelled more than five-fold to $332 billion by 2003.

The sudden surge in subprime mortgages and the securities based on them was not the only reason for over-optimistic credit ratings being given to the securities. Those who issued mortgage-backed securities "would 'shop' the securities at each of the three major rating entities and have the securities rated by the one that was willing to give the best rating." These credit-rating agencies were among the many contributors to the financial crisis by their insufficient caution in giving the new and untested securities favorable ratings.

Mortgages made under the Community Reinvestment Act were especially vulnerable during the housing downturn, to the detriment of both borrowers and lenders. For example, lending done under Community Reinvestment Act criteria, according to a quarterly report in October 2008, constituted only 7 percent of the total mortgage lending by the Bank of America, but constituted 29 percent of its losses on mortgages.

Even existing home buyers who did *not* have either subprime mortgages or adjustable-rate mortgages were nevertheless affected indirectly by the rising interest rates, because those higher interest rates caused rising home prices to suddenly turn into falling home prices. Therefore many home buyers, regardless of what kind of mortgage they had, could find the value of their home falling below the amount that they owed on the mortgage. That could confront them, as well as others, with a painful question: "Why continue to pay off a $500,000 mortgage on a home that is now worth only $350,000?"

In short, even some people who could afford to pay off their mortgages were now faced with incentives to stop doing so. People who had borrowed against the equity in their homes were of course at increased risk of finding that what they owed now exceeded the value of the remaining equity in their home, when they had both a mortgage to pay and a home-equity loan to repay. Here too were people who were *not* trapped by circumstances beyond their control but who chose risky ways of getting money and lost.

Home buyers in a variety of circumstances now had reasons to default on their mortgages— and they proceeded to do so, whether they had to or whether they simply chose to. This set in motion a sequence of events— beginning with rising rates of defaults and foreclosures, followed by declining values of financial institutions' assets based on the declining values of the mortgages they held. Those who owned stock in those financial institutions saw the value of their stock decline and some financial institutions on the other side of the Atlantic suffered heavy losses because of their investment in securities based on the value of American home mortgages.

The spread of financial disaster from local housing markets to national and international financial markets was much like a heavy rainfall high in the mountains, filling a thousand little creeks and streams that empty into a big river, ultimately flooding people living far downstream from the source of the water. Perhaps better levees might have saved the people downstream. But that does not change the fact that the flood originated in heavy rainfalls in the mountains. In the case of the housing market collapse, much has been made of the claim that there was inadequate regulatory agency oversight of the financial markets that turned home mortgages into esoteric Wall Street securities, which added to the risk. But these securities would have remained secure if people had continued to make their monthly mortgage payments.

It was ultimately the skyrocketing rates of mortgage delinquencies and defaults that were like the heavy rain in the mountains that caused the flooding downstream. As

Professor Stanley Liebowitz of the University of Texas at
Dallas put it: "From the current handwringing, you'd think
that the banks came up with the idea of looser underwriting
standards on their own, with regulators just asleep on the
job." Government was not passively inefficient. It was
actively zealous in promoting risky mortgage lending
practices.

Regulators

Widespread calls for more or better regulation do not come
to grips with the fact that there is no such thing as generic
"regulation." The regulation of Fannie Mae and Freddie Mac
by the Office of Federal Housing Enterprise Oversight
(OFHEO) was radically different from the regulation of banks
by various agencies that forced these banks into quota lending
and lower loan approval standards. These latter regulators
micro-managed mortgage standards while the former simply
held Fannie Mae and Freddie Mac to the existing accounting
rules, which they were violating. More important, those
regulators who pushed for lower mortgage approval standards
were doing what politicians wanted done, while OFHEO, by
holding Fannie Mae and Freddie Mac to the accounting rules,
was limiting the scope of these hybrid enterprises' operations,
bringing down on OFHEO the wrath of Senator Kit Bond and
Congressman Barney Frank, among others.

As we have already seen, government regulation and
intervention have been at the heart of the conditions that
set the stage for the current housing market disaster. That
does not mean that all regulation must be futile or
counterproductive. What it does mean is that the specifics of
any proposed regulation are crucial. Among these specifics
must be answers to such questions as: Regulate with what
powers? With what insulation from political interference?

With what accountability for what results? Such specifics would tell us much more than political rhetoric about a need for more generic "regulation."

There is already overlapping regulation of banks and other lending institutions by various federal agencies with varying jurisdictions and agendas, and a substantial portion of the lending institutions are regulated by state agencies. Moreover, mortgages as they pass from banks to Wall Street firms that bundle them into stocks and bonds pass from the jurisdiction of bank regulators into the jurisdiction of the Securities and Exchange Commission. Any hope of consistent coordination among all these overlapping regulatory organizations seems almost Utopian.

Those who speak of regulation in the abstract not only overlook how radically different one kind of regulation can be from another, they seldom bother to consider how many individual regulators there are to oversee how many varied lenders with ever growing kinds of complex and exotic lending arrangements. "At the peak of California's housing boom," according to one study, "no more than 30 state examiners watched over nearly 5,000 consumer finance companies," with the net result that mortgage companies "could expect an examination from state regulators about once every four years." That is longer than it took the housing market to go from boom to bust. Moreover, many of these regulators "felt pressure from local politicians to keep mortgage credit flowing freely to their constituents."

A question can also be raised as to whether members of the general public who enter the housing market are better off being told to rely on the government's protecting their interests— which, if done thoroughly, might require regulators as numerous as the hordes of Genghis Khan, each with a degree in accounting and some with degrees in law and economics as well— or to be told frankly that they had better watch their backs themselves. In other words, is the illusion of government protection better than *caveat emptor?* It all depends on the specifics, not on the generalities of political rhetoric.

ECONOMIC AND POLITICAL ADJUSTMENTS

The market's adjustments to the bursting of the housing bubble took place quickly and in predictable ways. In California, for example, the mixtures of homes purchased shifted toward what were, for California, less expensive homes. Homes costing less than half a million dollars were just 43 percent of all homes sold in California in 2007 but became 78 percent of all homes sold there the following year. In short, people were learning to stay within what their incomes could afford.

Although the median down payment during the housing boom was a record low 12 percent of the sales price in California in 2006, after the riskiness of low down payments became painfully clear to both borrowers and lenders in the wake of the housing bust, the median down payment rose to the traditional 20 percent level in 2008. The proportion of California home buyers who made no down payment at all dropped from 18 percent in 2007 to 3 percent in 2008, the lowest proportion in years.

The proportion of interest-only, adjustable-rate mortgages in the state also fell, from 16 percent of all mortgages in 2007 to 2 percent in 2008. Even first-time home buyers, who had financed 24 percent of their housing purchases with interest-only, adjustable rate mortgages at the height of the housing boom in 2005, financed only 2 percent of their home purchases that way in 2008. The old-fashioned fixed-rate, 30-year mortgage made a dramatic comeback, rising from just 55 percent of all mortgages in the state in 2005 to more than 90 percent of all California mortgages in 2008.

There were correspondingly large changes in the use of second mortgages. More than 60 percent of first-time home buyers in California had used second mortgages to purchase their homes in 2006 but that fell to 12 percent just two years later.

National trends were similar. Adjustable-rate mortgages, which were 35 percent of all mortgages in 2004, were down to 10 percent of all mortgages by 2007. While the total amount lent in subprime mortgages nationwide was nearly $140 billion in the fourth quarter of 2006, that fell to less that $20 billion in the fourth quarter of 2007. According to the *New York Times*, "lenders have become more cautious about whom they will lend to," and both refinancing and mortgage insurance now had more stringent requirements that borrowers must meet.

In short, the market learns— even if only the hard way— and adjusts with remarkable speed, when staring financial ruin in the face is the alternative. The question is whether politicians and government bureaucrats learn, especially when they pay no price for being wrong, and are able to deflect blame toward the market with denunciations of "greed," "Wall Street" or whatever other convenient scapegoats are available.

The Politics of Blame

In addition to the more or less ad hoc scapegoating of others, many of the architects of the lower mortgage lending standards at the heart of the housing boom and bust more systematically created scapegoats by summoning before Congressional committees various business leaders or federal employees to be denounced on nationwide television or before other members of the mass media. As the *New York Times* reported in September 2008: "Almost every member of the Senate Banking Committee wagged a finger at what they described as Wall Street's greed and lax regulatory oversight." This is the committee chaired by Senator Christopher Dodd. It was much the same story in hearings before the House Financial Services Committee— chaired by Congressman Barney Frank— in February 2009, where "the leaders of some of the country's largest banks endured hours of hectoring Wednesday by indignant lawmakers," as the *Los Angeles Times* reported.

Often those summoned before these committees to be publicly browbeaten or humiliated on television were in no position to answer in kind, whether because their jobs and their agencies' appropriations were at risk or because they were leaders of private businesses currently under federal regulation or which could be singled out for adverse new legislation.

This was just one of the ways in which Washington politicians demonstrated their understanding that the best defense is a good offense. Senator Christopher Dodd said: "I have a lot of questions about where was the administration over the last eight years." Often the Bush administration had sought increased power to rein in Fannie Mae and Freddie Mac during those years, while Senator Dodd fought adamantly against granting such powers.

Senator Dodd also blamed Federal Reserve Board chairman Alan Greenspan for the mortgage crisis, even though Greenspan had warned against the riskiness of policies that Dodd had defended in the name of "affordable housing." According to Senator Dodd in 2007, after the housing bubble had burst, Alan Greenspan "seemed to encourage the development and use of adjustable-rate mortgages that today are defaulting and going into foreclosure at record rates." But adjustable-rate mortgages have been the norm in Europe for decades, without causing a mortgage crisis. Lax lending standards used to meet "affordable housing" quotas were the key to the American mortgage crisis. That many of those who could not meet the regular American standards for a 30-year fixed-rate mortgage resorted to adjustable-rate, often subprime, mortgages was an effect, rather than a cause.*

While attacking Alan Greenspan, Senator Dodd continued to defend Fannie Mae and Freddie Mac. In February 2008, long after the housing bubble bust and its spreading damage was well underway, Senator Dodd said "we have sat through hours of hearings over the years with witnesses repeatedly raising alarm bells about the risks Fannie and Freddie pose to the financial system." But now these government-sponsored enterprises were "the only part of the housing finance system where credit is still flowing." Thus, while the financial system was now "under siege," Dodd said, it was Fannie Mae and Freddie Mac "that are riding to the rescue."

That private financial institutions, which were risking their own money, were reluctant to continue extending credit as freely as before under dire new conditions, while government-sponsored enterprises that could pass their risks on to the taxpayers were still going full steam ahead

---

*These new (to many Americans) mortgages grew to prominence at a time of unusually low interest rates that made the purchase of a home look more affordable than it was to less experienced people, who may not have been aware of how substantially their monthly mortgage payment would increase. Variations like below market "teaser" rates that might last for a matter of months added to the difference between initial monthly mortgage payments and the payments that would have to be made later.

was not surprising, much less a reason for congratulating them for getting in deeper, ultimately requiring hundreds of billions of dollars in bailouts. Yet Senator Dodd acted as if those who had issued the warnings he had consistently rejected were now discredited by the continued risky lending of Fannie Mae and Freddie Mac.

In reality, the government ended up taking over both of these enterprises and, in January 2009, the Congressional Budget Office estimated that covering Fannie Mae's and Freddie Mac's losses would cost the government $238 billion for the year. That was *before* the two enterprises requested an additional $70 billion. Altogether, the bailouts of Fannie Mae and Freddie Mac would cost the taxpayers more than the bailouts of Bank of America, Citigroup, J.P. Morgan Chase, and Wells Fargo *combined*.

In July 2008, the *Wall Street Journal* reported: "On Friday, Senate Banking Chairman Christopher Dodd (D., Conn.) declared that Fannie and Freddie are 'fundamentally strong,' that fears about their capital are overwrought, and that 'this is not a time to be panicking about this. These are viable, strong institutions.'" A week later, an editorial in the *Wall Street Journal* said "In any other business, Mr. Dodd would be begging forgiveness." But, in politics, the ability to brazen out your mistakes can be a crucial skill for the survival of a career.

Congressman Barney Frank likewise went on the offensive after the mortgage bust. In 2007, Congressman Frank said in the *Financial Times* of London that "the subprime crisis demonstrates the serious negative economic and social consequences that result from too little regulation." The financial crisis was caused by "bad decisions that were made by people in the private sector," Congressman Frank said in 2008, "thanks to a conservative philosophy that says the market knows best." "We are in a worldwide crisis now because of excessive deregulation," he said. According to Barney Frank, "mortgages made and sold in the unregulated sector led to the crisis."

The theme that the unregulated market was the source of the financial crisis was echoed by others, including Senator Charles Schumer:

> These unprecedented events have made it clear to the country what many of us have been saying for some time. We are in the midst of the greatest financial crisis since the Great Depression. After 8 years of deregulatory zeal by the Bush administration, an attitude of "the market can do no wrong" has led it down a short path to economic recession.

In the wake of the housing bust, Congressman Barney Frank and Senator Christopher Dodd, as chairmen of the House and Senate committees most involved in the housing market— and long-time promoters of the very policies that led to the housing boom and bust— were all over the media, where they were treated as experts, able to explain the problems and provide solutions.

Television financial reporter Maria Bartiromo was one of the few to challenge either Senator Dodd or Congressman Frank on their own roles in the housing mortgage crisis. After Congressman Frank gave his views on the causes and cure of the crisis, there was this exchange:

> *With all due respect, congressman, I saw videotapes of you saying in the past: "Oh, let's open up the lending. The housing market is fine."*
> No, you didn't see any such tapes.
>
> *I did. I saw them on TV.*
> Yeah, well, I never said open up the housing market, the market is fine. . . .
>
> *So whose fault is this?*
> The right-wing Republicans who took the position that regulation was always bad, the market was self-correcting,

and you should not have any restrictions on the free flow of capital.

This revisionist history ignored both the ill-advised and the well-advised interventions of the Bush administration, including their attempts to get stronger regulatory constraints put on Fannie Mae and Freddie Mac— attempts rejected by both Barney Frank in the House of Representatives and Christopher Dodd in the Senate, among others in Congress who obstructed those attempts.

On the Republican side, Senator Kit Bond, who had also tried to obstruct the regulators overseeing Fannie Mae and Freddie Mac, now came out in favor of "a new regulator with more expansive powers to oversee the two mortgage government-sponsored enterprises, Fannie Mae and Freddie Mac, if they continue to exist," adding that this was "a long overdue and necessary step." Moreover, he said that OFHEO "did not examine, did not look at the practices" that Fannie Mae and Freddie Mac had engaged in and that OFHEO had said "that these were sound operations." But it was precisely OFHEO's cracking down on Fannie Mae that had aroused Senator Bond's wrath in the past. Revisionist history has been bipartisan. A front-page article in the *St. Louis Post-Dispatch* recalled the facts, in contrast to Senator Bond's version, under the title "Bond's Tough Talk on Fannie, Freddie Rings Hollow to Some."

Political "Solutions"

Short-sighted suggestions of solutions to the housing crisis have also been bipartisan. Democratic Senator Barbara Boxer wanted more government intervention in the housing market. "Allow bankruptcy judges to modify loans on principal residences," Senator Boxer said— and Congressman John Conyers and Senator Richard Durbin introduced legislation to do just that. Senator Harry Reid endorsed the same idea. How empowering judges to void contracts would affect the future willingness of lenders to lend to millions of other people was a subject not addressed. It was a classic example of politicians "solving" one problem without regard to how many new problems that solution created.

The same short-sighted perspective was apparent when Republican Senator Mitch McConnell suggested "providing government-backed, 4% fixed mortgages to any credit-worthy borrower." Professor Edward Glaeser of Harvard, a specialist in the economics of housing markets, said the Republicans' plan would be both "wildly expensive and ineffective."

Senator Dodd's solution to the housing boom and bust was very much like his advocacy of what brought on the boom and bust— specify an end result, with no consideration of its ramifications. The mantra of "home ownership" was now joined by the mantra of "foreclosure mitigation." How people got into a situation where they faced foreclosure, or what would happen to housing markets after government intervention in foreclosures, were not matters addressed. However, the additional arbitrary goal did not replace the previous arbitrary goal. In sponsoring legislation to replace the existing regulator of Fannie Mae and Freddie Mac with a new regulatory agency, Senator Dodd said this would allow these government-sponsored enterprises to "better meet their mission of providing a source of affordable financing for homeownership."

Congressman Barney Frank likewise introduced legislation in the House of Representatives to save people facing foreclosure, with their financial responsibility to be mitigated by either the taxpayers or the lenders. Putting the cost of people's mistakes on other people hardly seems reasonable after the fact, and even less so as a prospective policy to discourage future mistakes.

Considering how quickly people in California drastically reduced their use of "creative" financing schemes when they had to pay the consequences, the case for sheltering people from consequences with federal legislation is by no means obvious. Unlike the bailouts of financial institutions, where the argument could be made that the shrinkage of credit if these institutions collapsed would hurt the whole economy, no such claim could be made for preventing mortgage foreclosures. While the decline of housing prices may be painful for their current owners, these declining prices make home purchases more affordable to prospective buyers— the very goal that politicians have been claiming to be pursuing for years. Yet affordable housing through the operations of the marketplace provides no political benefit to elected officials and elicits no support from them.

In the prevailing vision, foreclosure is a "problem" with a political "solution" and the people facing foreclosure are "victims"— and, needless to say, it is politically incorrect to "blame the victim." Unfortunately, facts from the world of reality tell a different story. Changing the terms of mortgage loans to help borrowers who are behind in their payments has not proven to be the end of the story. As *The Economist* magazine reported in February 2009: "Of 73,000 loans modified in the first quarter of last year, 43% were again delinquent eight months later."

Foreclosure is not something that just happens to people, like being struck by lightning. Foreclosure is the end result of a process that borrowers and lenders entered into in the past and that more borrowers and lenders will enter into in the future. An arbitrary intervention at some point in time in this ongoing process has to be assessed not only in terms of its justification as of that moment, given the choices that people made in the past, but also in terms of what incentives and constraints are created for those who consider entering that process in the future.

Almost certainly such political interventions will make lenders more reluctant to lend when their chances of getting their money back are reduced by the prospect of more political interventions in the years ahead. As a result, borrowers are likely to find it harder to get mortgage loans and the loans are likely to carry higher interest rates, in order to cover the increased risk of more political interventions. In short, the costs of bad decisions made in the past will result in more onerous terms for future borrowers, who had nothing to do with the decisions of others in the past.

Why those who made those decisions should be spared the consequences, and those who had nothing to do with their mistakes should be forced to suffer the consequences, is a question seldom raised, much less answered. The political answer is of course that elected officials have every incentive to hand out favors with the taxpayers' money.

BAILOUTS AND "STIMULUS"

As the housing market continued to decline in 2008, taking down with it the stock market and major financial institutions, some of which went bankrupt, while unemployment increased, Congress voted $700 billion to be spent under the Troubled Asset Relief Program (TARP) in the last months of the Bush administration, ostensibly to rescue financial institutions— and later, during the Obama administration, Congress passed legislation appropriating another nearly $800 billion "stimulus" package to try to revive the economy.

The rationale of the first bailout, TARP, was to prevent more financial institutions from collapsing, which could reduce the availability of credit, on which demand, output and employment depended. Banks across the country received millions of dollars each and some received billions. As of February 2009, the largest recipients of TARP money included J.P. Morgan Chase ($25 billion), Wells Fargo ($25 billion), AIG ($40 billion), Bank of America ($45 billion) and Citigroup ($50 billion). However, the government financial institution bailout money soon began to be spent for other things, such as bailing out General Motors and other non-financial enterprises.

Although many in Congress professed to be shocked at the way the money had been used for things different from what it had been said to be for, such a change was not unprecedented— nor even surprising, given the political incentives and given the history of government spending in many places and times. As far back as 1776, Adam Smith warned that a fund set aside by the British government for paying off the national debt was "an obvious and easy expedient" to be "misapplied" to other purposes. The next great classical economist, David Ricardo, objected to a similar fund in his time, on grounds that "we have, I fear, neither wisdom enough, nor virtue enough" for such a plan. Later, he said that this fund "has encouraged expenditure" and called it a "delusion" and "deceitful."

There may have been a more realistic understanding of the incentives and constraints of politics back in what are sometimes called "earlier and simpler times." Perhaps it is our time that is more naive in its expectations of politicians and government.

In today's emphasis on rescuing people arbitrarily singled out to be given the taxpayers' money, seldom has there been much discussion of homeowners who got themselves in over their heads with risky financial arrangements, not to mention speculators who had profited greatly from the boom and were now stuck with some of the inevitable losses that go with speculation. Both the bailout and the stimulus programs have serious problems, not always addressed seriously, including the timing of their effects and the dangers of inflation from so much unprecedented deficit spending, and— a key question— whether a "stimulus" program would in fact stimulate the economy.

Timing Problems

Even with the best intentions and the best expertise, it is not easy to know what the net effect of a given expenditure will be, much less when that effect will take place. Even in the normal course of actions taken by the Federal Reserve System to increase or reduce the money supply, the full effect may be delayed more than a year— and no one can be sure what the situation in the economy will be after a year or more has passed. An increase in the money supply begun when the economy has insufficient demand can take its full effect at a time when there are inflationary pressures, which the new infusion of money can aggravate.

Where the current large increases in government spending are said to be for infrastructure, the delayed impact may take an especially long time to be felt, since building almost anything can require complying with all sorts of federal, state and local rules involving environmental studies that must first be performed and hearings that must be held by various agencies, where all sorts of objections must be considered and adjudicated. Predicting when all the money currently being appropriated will actually be spent is especially challenging under these conditions.

If the money appropriated for infrastructure were spent for repairs of existing roads, bridges and the like, instead of for building new structures, the money might well enter the economy sooner and more predictably. However, the very reason for the widespread neglect of the maintenance and repair of infrastructure is that political incentives favor building new things, rather than repairing or maintaining existing things. Building a plaza, a community center or a marina creates occasions for ribbon-cutting ceremonies that provide valuable favorable publicity for elected officials. But there are no ribbon-cutting ceremonies for filling in potholes or repairing bridges and sewers.

Inflation

Regardless of when the "stimulus" money takes effect in the economy, the sheer size of the stimulus package ensures that its effect will be huge, whether for good or ill. The money involved seems certain to exceed a trillion dollars and may be multiple trillions before it is all over. Within living memory, there was a time when the entire national output of the United States was less than a trillion dollars. Today, there are many countries— in fact, *most* of the countries in the world— whose entire national output still does not reach a trillion dollars.

Since many people have trouble grasping what a trillion means, one way to visualize it is that a trillion seconds ago, no one on this planet could read or write. The ancient Chinese dynasties and the Roman Empire had not yet come into being. None of the founders of Christianity, Judaism or Islam had yet been born. That was a trillion *seconds* ago— and we are talking about trillions of dollars.

In addition to the vastness of the stimulus package, it is not simply spending but *deficit* spending. The government already had a deficit before any of this money was appropriated, so this is new money, essentially created out of thin air. The potential for inflation is huge. More than that, even Wall Street does not have an unlimited amount of money, so that borrowing money through the sale of government bonds absorbs funds that would otherwise be available to go into private investments that create private jobs.

After twenty years of very low rates of inflation, it may be too easy for the public to forget what dangers inflation can pose. At least half of the American population today had either not been born, or not yet reached adulthood, at the time of the "stagflation" of the 1970s, when the economy suffered both high inflation and stagnant growth at the same time, with high unemployment and interest rates in double digits. Many of today's Americans may even be unaware of the wrenching economic problems of the early 1980s— widespread business failures and unemployment— as the Federal Reserve followed restrictive monetary policies to break the back of inflation.

In the process, Federal Reserve Chairman Paul Volcker became one of the most hated men in America, and President Ronald Reagan saw his popularity in the polls plummet for supporting what Volcker was doing. Eventually it worked and the country enjoyed two decades of economic growth with low inflation afterwards. But no one at the time knew when "eventually" would be, and many suffered in the meantime. They would undoubtedly have suffered even more had inflation continued to rise out of control. But the existing pain was what people felt.

Inflation is not the only legacy of runaway government spending. A growing national debt can be regarded as the ghost of Christmas past. At one time, Keynesian economists downplayed the problem of running up a huge national debt, saying, "We owe it to ourselves," since most of the government securities that constitute the national debt were sold to Americans. It was not quite that simple, even back in the heyday of Keynesian economics.* But, as of 2007, approximately 45 percent of the publicly held American national debt is held by individuals and organizations in other countries. This means that future generations of Americans will have to ship trillions of dollars' worth of their output to China and other countries to whom that debt is owed.

"Stimulation" of the Private Sector

A "stimulus" is supposed to stimulate somebody or something. In other words, stimulus spending— even on the unprecedented scale in the current stimulus package— is not by itself supposed to restore the economy to prosperity and rising employment. As the President of the United States and other spokesmen for the Obama administration repeat endlessly, this spending is supposed to stimulate other spending, as the money works its way through the economy. In other words, government sector spending is supposed to stimulate business and consumer spending in the private sector.

The idea sounds fine, as most political ideas do. But the real question is: Is that what has actually happened? Is that what usually happens?

At the end of 2008, after hundreds of billions of dollars of the Bush administration's stimulus package and TARP bailout money had been spent in the preceding months,

---

*See my *Basic Economics*, 3rd edition, pp. 404–405.

what was actually happening in the private sector? According to the *Wall Street Journal*, business spending on equipment and software in the last quarter of 2008 "fell 27.8%, the worst in a half-century. Spending on durable goods fell 22.4%. The only spending that increased was by government." Apparently consumers as well as businesses were holding on to their money. So were banks, as the *New York Times* reported:

> With new capital, Congress and the Bush administration hoped, banks would resume normal lending to businesses and consumers. But worried banks are holding onto the money, so there has been scant benefit to the economy from the government help to the banks.

The velocity of circulation of money fell faster than it had in 50 years. When money moves more *slowly* through the economy than before, that does not sound like stimulus but more like sedation or paralysis. Calling something a stimulus does not make it a stimulus.

The same kinds of trends continued into the new year. The Associated Press reported that January 2009 was Wall Street's "worst January ever," with both the Dow Jones Industrial Average and Standard & Poor's 500 index "setting record percentage drops for January."

Those who believe that January's economic trends are a good indicator of what to expect for the year as a whole have history on their side. According to the Associated Press: "Since 1950, there have been only five times when the January Barometer got it wrong in a big way." The *Wall Street Journal*, owned by Dow Jones, reported that the Dow Jones Industrial Average decline in January was the worst January in its 113-year history and "the fifth consecutive month of declines. The 31% decline over the five months was the sharpest since the five months ended December 1937." That was, of course, during the Great Depression of the

1930s. In February 2009, the Dow Jones Industrial Average fell to *one-half* of where it had been just 16 months earlier.

Amid a chorus of demands that government "do something" about the economic downturn, there has been remarkably little interest in comparing what happens when government does something and when it does not. Nor has there been much attention paid to the fact that generic "something" is as meaningless as generic "regulation" or generic "change." Government can only do something *specific*— and just what that specific something is determines whether it is likely to make things better or worse. In the long history of the United States, it has been only since the Great Depression of the 1930s that the federal government has intervened in the economy in response to an economic downtown. Since markets recovered on their own faster from previous depressions, it is by no means unambiguously clear that an imperative to "do something" speeds recovery.

One of the things that government can do more effectively than any other institution is create uncertainty, simply because government decisions constrain everyone else's decisions. For example, with Senator Barbara Boxer blithely talking about empowering judges to rewrite mortgage contracts to suit the judges' notions, would that encourage or discourage lenders to write more mortgages, when they would have no idea what their chances were of getting their money back, in accordance to the terms of the contract made with the borrower? Many political quick fixes pay little or no attention to how those quick fixes change incentives and constraints on future behavior.

Far more momentous than Senator Boxer's suggestion have been the ad hoc— and therefore unpredictable— policies at the end of the Bush administration and the beginning of the Obama administration. First there was the

Troubled Asset Relief Program, submitted to Congress in 2008 by Chairman Ben Bernanke of the Federal Reserve Board and Secretary of the Treasury Henry Paulson, as "a two-and-a-half-page legislation, with no mention of oversight and few restrictions on the use" of the $700 billion involved, as monetary economist John B. Taylor of Stanford University characterized it. A survey of securities firms and banks showed that 94 percent of them "found the TARP lacking in clarity about its operations." Moreover, bailout decisions in general— rescuing Bear Stearns but letting Lehman Brothers collapse— provided no basis for financial markets to figure out what the rules or principles of such decisions were, leading to uncertainties about the government's interventions.

The point here is not that these particular decisions were bad in themselves. Everyone has to make ad hoc judgment calls at some point or other. But a *government's* ad hoc decisions provide no reliable framework for the decisions to be made by millions of other people subject to the government's rules, when those rules are difficult to discern. One of the hardest things for a market to adjust to is uncertainty, whether it is uncertainty about how judges will change mortgage contracts when given a free hand to do so or— even more important— what new government interventions in the financial markets will strike like a bolt from the blue. When money appropriated to rescue financial institutions began to be spent to bail out General Motors, that signalled ad hoc decision-making, whatever the merits or demerits of bailing out General Motors might be.

Still more uncertainty was generated by the new Obama administration, when the President announced on February 9, 2009 that the next day Secretary of the Treasury Timothy Geithner "will be announcing some very clear and specific plans for how we are going to start loosening up credit once again." But when Secretary Geithner then appeared on nationwide television the next day with no concrete policy but only vague generalities, the stock market took a nosedive. Even newspapers generally sympathetic to the administration— the *New York Times*, the *Washington Post*, and the *St. Louis Post-Dispatch*, for example— complained of the lack of specifics. A *New York Times* editorial referred to the "lead-balloon reception of Mr. Geithner's plan"; *Washington Post* writers said such things as "after watching his debut this week, I don't see how he could get much worse" and "it contributed to the very public anxiety and investor uncertainty that Geithner criticized."

With the Bush administration, the uncertainty was over what they were going to do. With the Obama administration, the uncertainty is over whether they themselves know what they are going to do.

Perhaps the housing market collapse and its repercussions so threatened the whole financial system that government intervention was imperative, in order to prevent a domino effect of collapsing financial institutions and a drying up of the credit on which the whole economy depends. But, if so, that would not justify spending vast sums of money on automobile companies and innumerable pet projects from coast to coast. Moreover, an urgent need to prop up tottering financial institutions is completely incompatible with arranging the spending in such a way that most of it will not be done within a year of the hastily passed stimulus bill of 2009.

Despite the rhetoric of urgency and the great haste with which this legislation was rushed through Congress to spend unprecedented sums of money, the actual programs and policies created are very *slow*-acting. In February 2009, the Congressional Budget Office estimated that it would be September 2010 before even three-quarters of the money would be spent. *The Economist* magazine commented: "Too much of the boost to demand is backloaded to 2010 and beyond." This is a very strange combination of unprecedented haste to pass legislation appropriating money that would be spent at a very slow pace.

Why there has been such *haste* to pass a *slow*-acting bill is a question to return to in the last chapter.

Chapter 4

Housing Mystiques and Housing Mistakes

The current housing crisis and its economic repercussions, within the United States and beyond, have evolved within a set of assumptions and beliefs that are part of an older and wider vision. That older and wider vision has remained as little examined by many of those who have believed it as has the set of ideas behind the policies that created the current housing crisis.

Housing is too important in most people's lives to expect it to always be discussed dispassionately. "Home" is, after all, a word with emotional overtones, quite aside from its physical or economic significance. It would be hard to understand the evolution of housing policies in the United States over the years without understanding the framework of values, beliefs and assumptions— in short, the vision— on which they are founded. We have already seen one aspect of the prevailing vision, namely the notion that unaffordable housing prices are produced by the free market and that making housing affordable requires government intervention. However, there are other aspects of the prevailing vision which would also require government intervention, and those also require an examination that they seldom receive.

This is not to say that sheer idealism drives housing policies. Regardless of how sincerely a particular vision may be conceived and believed by some, both politicians and special interests can use the prevailing vision to advance their own interests. It was, for example, the *National Real Estate Investor* magazine which said in 2002:

> A new report by the Millennial Housing Commission confirms what advocates of affordable housing have claimed: More Americans are finding it impossible to find affordable housing.

Heartening as it might be to imagine that real estate investors were worried about people unable to afford housing, it is hard to overlook the possibility that they might also be interested in how "affordable housing" programs can create opportunities for real estate investors. Similarly, when the bipartisan Millennial Housing Commission, appointed by Congress in 2000, presented a picture of a *national* lack of affordable housing, requiring a variety of national programs, it is hard to overlook what political opportunities such national— that is, federal government— programs would present to Congressional Democrats and Republicans alike, to visibly dramatize a concern for the less fortunate with new laws and new appropriations of the taxpayers' money.

Other aspects of the prevailing vision have promoted many other government policies, from the local level to the national level. As with the affordability argument, we must compare the vision with the empirical reality.

VISIONS AND REALITIES

Visions may be generated by all sorts of people for all sorts of reasons, including genuine concerns for the well-being of other people and of the country as a whole. But once a particular vision has become widely accepted, so many people may have such a vested interest— whether financial, political or ideological— that the vision can become remarkably resistant to the facts of the real world. Visions of housing have long been classic examples.

Housing and Behavior

The Millennial Housing Commission set forth a vision of housing that has been prevalent for at least a century:

> Decent and affordable housing has a demonstrable impact on family stability and the life outcomes of children. Decent housing is an indispensable building block of healthy neighborhoods, and thus shapes the quality of community life. . . . Better housing can lead to better outcomes for individuals, communities, and American society as a whole.

It is certainly true that neighborhoods with better housing also usually have more stable families, better educated children and lower crime rates. But statisticians have long pointed out that correlation is not causation, though that may be the most often ignored lesson in statistics. American families that travel to Monaco are probably better off in many ways than families that never leave the United States. But that does not mean that the federal government should subsidize trips to Monaco or expect social benefits if they do.

The presumed causal role of housing in behavior patterns has a long pedigree. Nineteenth century reporter-reformer Jacob Riis called the "places and domiciles" of New York's rundown lower east side "nurseries of crime." He strongly favored slum-clearance programs, though noting in passing that in many cases "the police had to drag the tenants out by force" before the demolition could begin— which might suggest that these tenants had a different view of their best interests than that of Riis and the reformers he inspired. Yet this vision of the causal role of housing in social behavior, and of the superior wisdom of third party observers, has persisted to this day, despite an accumulation of far more evidence to the contrary than was available in Jacob Riis' time.

Perhaps the most dramatic evidence to the contrary was provided in the twentieth century by massive transfers of people from crime-ridden slums into brand new public housing projects— which quickly became new centers of crime and quickly deteriorated into new slums. Even in Jacob Riis' time, he noted that some people "carry their slums with them wherever they go." But somehow this did not dim his crusading zeal for slum clearance, much less change his over-all vision of the role of housing in social outcomes. Nor have the repeated, massive and multiple failures of public housing projects in later times caused others to abandon that vision.

Even after many public housing projects had become such social disaster areas that they have been demolished with explosives, what was not demolished were the assumptions that had led to such hugely costly failures in the first place. When that particular way of trying to change people's behavior by moving them into better housing failed, it simply led to other ways of attempting to do the same thing, such as issuing Section 8 housing vouchers to enable some people to go rent in middle class neighborhoods, where they could not otherwise afford to live.

Bitter complaints about the behavior of such people in their new surroundings by neighbors, landlords and law enforcement have largely fallen on deaf ears, and the vision has remained unchanged. Apparently those with direct personal experience must be wrong and a vision shared among the elites must be right. Some complaints have been dismissed as "racism" when the voucher tenants have been black, but some of the bitterest complaints have come from black neighbors, who in many cases moved away from ghettos in order to get away from the very kinds of dysfunctional people that the government sends to live among them in their new neighborhoods. Not all voucher tenants are dysfunctional but it takes very few who are to make life miserable for their neighbors.

Nor has the vision of housing's effect on behavior been re-examined in light of the opposite phenomenon— namely, the existence of neighborhoods with older and unprepossessing housing, but with low crime rates and low rates of disease and other social pathology. In Jane Jacobs' classic, *The Death and Life of Great American Cities*, she recalled an Italian neighborhood in Boston that an urban planning expert described as "the worst slum in the city," but which his own data showed to have "among the lowest delinquency, disease and infant mortality rates in the city." Social dogmas and the visions behind them die hard, and sometimes they refuse to die at all, when those who have those visions pay no price for being wrong.

The vision that Jacob Riis had in the nineteenth century was still going strong in the Millennial Housing Commission's report in the twenty-first century. The only difference was that now it had more political muscle behind it, despite more empirical evidence against it. That vision now served to promote widespread government interventions in the housing market to create "affordable housing" and to protect people considered to be vulnerable, such as racial or ethnic minorities. The actual, counterproductive track record of government intervention as regards the affordability of housing has made no dent on the social vision behind such interventions. Nor has the evidence on the effects of government interventions on minorities been examined with any such scrutiny as might dim the enthusiasm for that activity.

This long-standing social crusading mentality has played a major role in pushing policies of lowered mortgage lending standards that led to the housing market collapse and its repercussions throughout the economy today.

While Democrats have been prominent in these crusades at both the local and national levels, some Republicans have been part of the picture as well. It was none other than President George W. Bush who said, in 2002: "We can put light where there's darkness, and hope where there's despondency in this country. And part of it is working together as a nation to encourage folks to own their own home." Six years later, when his own Secretary of the Treasury explained to him the magnitude of the economic disaster, he asked "How did we get here?" Apparently, neither he nor many others in politics and the media saw any connection between their housing crusades and the economic crisis now facing the nation.

Protecting Minorities

One of the driving forces behind the strong pressures brought to bear against financial institutions, to lend to people they were not lending to as often as to others, has been a widespread belief that lenders' existing standards and practices discriminated against non-white applicants for mortgage loans, whether intentionally or systemically. Statistical studies which seemed to support this view have been highly publicized in the media, accompanied by expressions of indignation and outrage, along with demands that government officials "do something" to put a stop to such discrimination. Criticisms of these studies receive little, if any, attention in the media.

However sincerely many people believe in the vision of racial discrimination as the explanation for differential rates of approval of mortgage loan applications, like other visions it can be useful to special interests, regardless of its empirical validity or lack of empirical validity. That vision is useful not only to politicians seeking the support of ethnic voting blocs, it is financially rewarding to a whole class of racial activists who have extracted literally millions of dollars each from financial institutions by raising claims of racial discrimination, especially when these institutions were seeking government permission for such things as mergers, acquisitions or the opening of new branches.

Such claims, if not withdrawn after financial and other concessions are made by the financial institutions, could take years to adjudicate, costing vastly more money by the delay than is required to buy off the claimants. Jesse Jackson has been prominent among those using this tactic and, as a result, acquiring millions of dollars in donations from financial institutions for various organizations he controls. But he has not been alone, by any means. The community activist organization ACORN (Association of Community Organizations for Reform Now) has been another. According to the *Los Angeles Times*:

> ACORN, for example, has used the CRA [Community Reinvestment Act] as leverage to compel banks to create pools of loans for low- and moderate-income families. Its efforts have generated about $6 billion in loans to these borrowers, while also generating funds for ACORN's nonprofit housing corporation. Supporters call that a win-win scenario; critics say it's legalized extortion.

Congressman Paul Broun is one of those critics. The banks in his district "couldn't expand their services and they couldn't put in ATM machines unless they would make these bad loans." Congressman Barney Frank, on the other hand, defended activists whose interventions had extracted money and other concessions from lending institutions. He characterized these activists as "people who are trying very hard to preserve some equity and some social justice," and as "people whose only crime was to offend powerful political interests because they cared about equity."

However irrelevant the empirical validity of claims of racial discrimination may be to those who use such claims to advance their own political or financial interests, the truth or falsity of these claims is crucial for the society as a whole.

The methods used in statistical studies that have been widely cited to claim that there is mortgage lending discrimination are based on comparing approval rates of mortgage loan applications between blacks and whites, or between blacks and Hispanics, on the one hand, compared to non-Hispanic whites on the other. However, the data in a 1991 study by the Federal Reserve System that set off a nationwide outcry against differences in mortgage loan approval rates between whites and non-whites nevertheless showed that most applicants of any race were approved. Among those applying for government-backed loans, the approval rates were 61 percent for blacks and 77 percent for whites. For conventional loans, the approval rates were 56 percent for blacks and 76 percent for whites. For refinancing loans, the approval rates were 61 percent for blacks and 74 percent for whites. So the issue is the cause of statistical differences in approval rates, not whether any group is shut out of the market.

Significantly, seldom do widely publicized racial comparisons include Asian Americans, even when data on Asian Americans are available in the same data from which black-white comparisons are made. This is a crucial omission, as we shall see, for including Asian Americans would undermine both the conclusions and the methods used to reach those conclusions.

In a mortgage loan approval process where innumerable factors affect outcomes, only those factors which these studies choose to take into account, and for which there are also statistics available, are studied. Moreover, large intergroup differences are found in virtually all the loan approval factors that are compared, such as income, the kind of housing for which financing is being sought, whether it is initial financing or refinancing being sought, home purchase loans or home improvement loans, and other differences. Loan approval rates vary with all these factors and with other factors, regardless of race, so that racial differences in these factors make racial differences in loan approval rates virtually inevitable, whether there is racial discrimination or not.

The 1991 empirical study by the Federal Reserve System that evoked widespread outcries against mortgage lending discrimination was very upfront about the shortcomings of the data:

> Differences in approval and denial rates among groups and neighborhoods revealed by the new data can be expected to raise questions about the adequacy and fairness of the home lending process. The data have important limitations, however, and care must be taken in drawing conclusions from observed lending patterns. Foremost among these limitations is a lack of information about factors that are important in determining the creditworthiness of applicants and the adequacy of the collateral offered as security for their loans. Without taking into account such information, one cannot determine whether individual applicants or applicants grouped by a common characteristic (such as race or gender) have been treated fairly.

Many in politics and the media, however, proceeded to do exactly what this study said could not be done. They took the data as virtual proof of racial discrimination in mortgage lending. An editorial in *USA Today* began "Getting turned down for a mortgage may have more to do with how you look than how much you make" and ended "How you look must not be allowed to determine where you live." An editorial in the *St. Louis Post-Dispatch* said:

> A report by the Federal Reserve Board gives weight to the charge that blacks, Hispanics and some other minorities are rejected for mortgage loans far more frequently than whites with comparable income. The study makes a strong case for fairer mortgage-lending standards. . . Federal bank regulators must now step in and insist that these institutions adopt strong measures to end discriminatory lending patterns.

The *St. Louis Post-Dispatch* also opined that "lending institutions are being far more conservative than they have to be in determining the creditworthiness of minorities." Subsequent default rates suggest otherwise.

It was not only in editorial comment, but in the way that news stories were presented, that made it appear that the Federal Reserve data proved racial discrimination. Many news accounts led off with statements pointing clearly to that conclusion. A front page news story in the *Wall Street Journal* began: "When it comes to buying a home, not all Americans are created equal. If you're black, it's twice as likely your mortgage application will be rejected as it is if you're white." A *New York Times* news story began: "The most comprehensive report on mortgage lending nationwide ever issued by the Government shows that even within the same income group whites are nearly twice as likely as blacks to get loans."

What many seemed to consider damning evidence was that blacks and whites with the same income still had different mortgage loan acceptance rates. Yet the very study they cited pointed out that "income is the only financial characteristic of the applicant" in the data that were used, and that "several consumer financial characteristics" enter into a decision to approve or disapprove a mortgage loan application, including "the proportion of the consumer's income that will need to be dedicated to the repayment of the proposed loan plus other outstanding debts, the level of equity (through the downpayment) that the consumer is able and willing to put into the property, the consumer's employment experience and prospects, and the consumer's history of repaying debts."

The wealth or net worth of mortgage loan applicants is also a factor. Blacks and whites with the same *income* have very different amounts of *wealth*. Census data show that even blacks in the highest income quintile have less than one-third the net worth of whites in the highest income quintile. Indeed, blacks in the highest income quintile have less net worth than whites in the second-highest income quintile. Therefore comparing black and white mortgage loan applicants with the same *income*, in order to see if there is discrimination, is still comparing apples and oranges in terms of one of the determinants of mortgage loan eligibility— namely, wealth or net worth. Not surprisingly, in view of history, there are greater differences between blacks and whites in inherited wealth than in current incomes.

Other data in the 1991 Federal Reserve study and a later 1992 study showed that whites were denied conventional home mortgage loans more often than Asian Americans. Later studies also showed that whites resorted to subprime loans more often than Asian Americans— but these facts were almost never reported in the media. What such omitted facts might imply was that financial and behavioral differences among groups can lead to differences in mortgage loan approval rates, among other things, whether or not race as such was the basis for approval or non-approval. But this inconvenient possibility was eliminated by leaving Asian Americans out of the picture. Credit history is another of the factors influencing mortgage loan approval, and credit ratings differ among groups. Just as whites average higher credit scores than blacks or Hispanics, so Asian Americans average higher credit scores than whites.

One of the few places in the press where any of these kinds of data were even mentioned was in an op-ed column in the *Atlanta Journal-Constitution*:

> Among blacks, 52 percent have credit scores that would classify them as subprime borrowers.
>
> In metro Atlanta, 49 percent of blacks wind up with a subprime mortgage.
>
> Among whites, 16 percent have managed their personal credit so poorly that they'd be classified as subprime borrowers.
>
> In metro Atlanta, 13 percent of whites end up with subprime mortgages. . . . Without question, more blacks (49 percent) than Hispanics (34 percent), more Hispanics than whites (13 percent) and more whites than Asians (10 percent) used subprime loans to buy a house.

Data like these are usually buried in ponderous research papers that the general public does not read.

It is no wonder that these plain facts are so seldom reported in most of the media. Such hard data would undermine the moral melodrama that is more in keeping with the prevailing vision and with the interests of politicians and activists. All too typical of media coverage was a *Washington Post* story that began: "About 29 percent of African Americans who bought or refinanced homes last year ended up with high-cost loans, compared with only about 10 percent of white Americans," according to what was described as "a consumer advocacy group's analysis of new data from 15 large national lenders."

A 2002 statistical study, done by a research organization for the Department of Housing and Urban Development, included credit histories among its variables and concluded: "More substantive conclusions, particularly with regard to implications for the existence of racial discrimination in mortgage lending, are hazardous." Differences in credit scores between groups are just one of the salient factors usually missing in statistical comparisons of mortgage loan approval rates or rates of using subprime mortgages.

Another Federal Reserve study of subprime borrowing in 2006, also using Home Mortgage Disclosure Act data, noted: "The HMDA data do not include many of the factors considered in credit underwriting and pricing." But such crucial caveats are seldom mentioned in most political and media alarms about statistical disparities in mortgage loan approval rates. This later Federal Reserve study showed a pattern similar to what earlier studies had shown, namely that "black and Hispanic borrowers are more likely, and Asians [sic] borrowers less likely, to obtain loans with prices above the pricing thresholds than are non-Hispanic white borrowers."

Including the differential mortgage loan approval rates between Asian Americans and whites shows that the same methods used to conclude that blacks are discriminated against in mortgage lending would also lead to the conclusion that whites are discriminated against in favor of Asian Americans, reducing this whole procedure to absurdity, since no one believes that banks are discriminating against whites. To continue believing in such statistical methods of determining discrimination would mean accepting empirical evidence when it fits the prevailing vision and rejecting it when it does not.

Not only the omission of data on white-Asian American differences in news accounts of racial differences in mortgage lending approval rates, but the way other data are presented, clearly indicate how supposedly straight news accounts lead readers toward a preconceived conclusion. For example, when loan approval rates are not cited, but loan denial rates are, that creates a larger statistical disparity, since most loans are approved. Even if 98 percent of blacks had their mortgage loan applications approved, if 99 percent of whites were approved then by quoting denial rates alone it could be said that blacks were rejected twice as often as whites.

Although this hypothetical example is only an illustration of the difference between citing loan approval rates and citing loan denial rates, the same principle has been very much in evidence in the real world. For example, a 1992 study of mortgage loan application outcome differences in the Boston area by the Federal Reserve Bank of Boston did not mention loan *approval* rates even once in its 71 pages. Instead, it gave loan *denial* rates among those blacks, Hispanics and whites who were comparable on a wider range of variables than in the 1991 study. These loan denial rates were 11 percent for whites and 17 percent for non-whites. The way this was reported was "even after controlling for financial, employment, and neighborhood characteristics, black and Hispanic mortgage applicants in the Boston metropolitan area are roughly 60 percent more likely to be turned down than whites."

It is certainly true that a 17 percent rejection rate is larger than an 11 percent rejection rate— 55 percent larger, which can be considered "roughly 60 percent" only by being very rough. But it is also true that the very same information could be conveyed by saying that there was simply a 6 percentage point difference in loan denial rates and that the great majority of both white and non-white applicants were approved among people who were comparable in some of the factors that go into mortgage lending decisions. But such careful distinctions were seldom, if ever, made in the media.

Again, news stories opened with statements that turned them into de facto editorials. The *Boston Globe*, for example, reported this study by beginning: "A landmark study released yesterday shows that banks in Greater Boston discriminate against black and Hispanic mortgage applicants, offering the most damning evidence to date of racial hurdles facing minority homebuyers." Under the headline "Boston Fed Finds Racial Discrimination In Mortgage Lending Is Still Widespread," a *Wall Street Journal* news story reported the Boston Federal Reserve study, with a comment from an unnamed "spokeswoman for the Office of the Comptroller of the Currency" who declared the study "definitive."

The head of the Federal Reserve Bank of Boston declared, "no more studies needed." But apparently the Federal Reserve Board in Washington did not consider this study the last word, for a later research paper from the Federal Reserve in Washington found the conclusions of the Boston Federal Reserve Bank "difficult to justify" in view of a re-examination of the same data.

Among others who did not find this study "definitive" was financial specialist Mark Zandi, who pointed out that blacks and Hispanics tended to buy lower-priced houses— and that these were precisely the kinds of houses whose prices were falling the fastest during the period of the survey, making such houses a more risky investment, regardless of who was buying them. Nobel-Prizewinning economist Gary Becker, who pioneered in the economics of discrimination, found the Boston Federal Reserve study, among others, had "serious methodological flaws" that "make them of dubious value in formulating social policy."

Whatever the empirical weaknesses of the evidence for attributing intergroup differentials in mortgage loan approval rates to racial discrimination, the *legal* case for lending discrimination has been much easier to make, given the standards used in civil rights law, where the existence of statistical disparities is enough to establish a *prima facie* case against the accused— after which the burden of proof shifts to the accused to prove his innocence.

When neither side can convincingly prove anything— as is often the case— the accused stands to lose, since the burden of proof has been shifted to the accused in such cases, contrary to the usual practice in civil cases, not to mention criminal cases. Moreover, the process costs of fighting a discrimination charge can be enormous, whether the charge is racial discrimination or sex discrimination. The Sears department store chain, for example, spent $20 million fighting a sex discrimination case for 15 years, even though the Equal Employment Opportunity Commission that brought charges against Sears did not produce even one woman, either currently or previously employed in any of Sears' hundreds of stores across the country, to claim that she personally had been discriminated against.

Statistics alone were enough to establish a *prima facie* case that kept the litigation going. Even though Sears eventually won in the Circuit Court of Appeals, few businesses could afford to spend the kind of money that Sears spent and endure years of bad publicity that go with accusations of discrimination. Most businesses— even large corporations like General Motors— have found it prudent to settle such cases out of court on whatever terms they can get. These settlements are then cited by activists and others as proof of widespread discrimination by race or sex.

Banks and other lending institutions are especially vulnerable, because they have to get the approval of government regulatory agencies in order to make business decisions that Sears and other businesses are free to make without government permission. Even if a bank might be willing to pay out vast sums of money to fight discrimination charges for years, federal regulatory agencies can hold up approval for that bank's mergers, acquisitions and other business decisions, pending the outcome of those cases.

In the wake of the highly publicized statistical studies of racial disparities in mortgage loan approval rates in the early 1990s that have already been quoted here, the Clinton administration went into action on a number of fronts. The first prosecution of a bank for racial discrimination in mortgage lending was made in 1992, when the Justice Department charged the Decatur Federal Savings & Loan Association with racial discrimination, based on statistical differences between mortgage loan approval rates between blacks and whites. According to the *Wall Street Journal*, "Decatur denied the charges and said it chose settlement over protracted litigation." Given the standards used by courts in such cases and the arbitrary powers of federal regulatory agencies to withhold their approval of various business decisions by banks, it is hard to imagine a bank doing otherwise.

A year later, the Federal Reserve Board refused to approve an application by the Shawmut National Corporation to acquire the New Dartmouth Bank, "because of the bank's record on racial fairness," as the *New York Times* put it. The bank had not been convicted of anything in a court of law but the Federal Reserve Board was not required to use such legal standards. After the Federal Reserve referred the case to the Justice Department, the mortgage subsidiary of Shawmut National Corporation settled out of court by agreeing to "pay at least $960,000 to compensate minority applicants who may have been unfairly denied loans," according to the *Washington Times*.

Attorney General Janet Reno warned other banks that those who "closely examine their lending practices and make necessary changes to eliminate discrimination" would "fare better in this department's stepped-up enforcement effort than those who do not." She said: "Do not wait for the Justice Department to come knocking."

After Shawmut's settlement, the Federal Reserve Board then withdrew its opposition to Shawmut's acquisition of the New Dartmouth Bank. In a column titled "How to Rob a Bank Legally," economist Paul Craig Roberts said: "Believe it or not, there were no individual complaints from minorities." Here, as in the Sears case, statistical disparities were enough for a lawsuit, even if there was not one flesh-and-blood human being who even claimed to have been discriminated against personally. In the case of a bank, just the existence of such a lawsuit can freeze the bank's ability to make and carry out business decisions that require the approval of government regulatory agencies.

With both regulatory agencies and law-enforcement agencies equating statistical disparities with discrimination, banks across the country began to settle cases out of court. Attorney General Janet Reno expanded the definition of discrimination, bringing a case against the Chevy Chase Federal Savings Bank because it did not have branches in minority neighborhoods. The bank settled, like many other banks. The *New York Times* reported: "Under the settlement, the Chevy Chase Federal Savings Bank will open new branches and mortgage offices in poor neighborhoods to help redress what the Justice Department called racial bias."

How much any of this actually helped blacks is another question entirely. Being granted loans because the bank needs to meet statistical targets— quotas— in order to keep federal agencies off their backs, rather than because you are likely to be able to repay the loans, is not unequivocally a benefit to the borrower. As already noted in Chapters 2 and 3, members of minority groups have been disproportionately represented among those who took out subprime mortgages with initially low "teaser" rates that were for many a financial trap.

Other aspects of government housing policies have likewise been of no benefit to minorities and have, in fact, been demonstrably detrimental. For example, skyrocketing housing prices in particular communities around the country with severe building restrictions hit blacks especially hard, even though many of these communities have been overwhelmingly liberal in their politics, with emphasis on their concern for minorities, the poor and children. In fact, however, each of these groups, for whom much concern has been expressed, have been precisely the groups disproportionately forced *out* of these high housing cost communities.

In San Francisco, for example, the black population has been cut in half since 1970. In an even shorter span of time, between the 1990 and 2000 censuses, four California counties— Los Angeles County, San Mateo County, and Alameda County, as well as San Francisco County— have had their black populations decline by more than ten thousand each, despite increases in the general populations of these counties. Nor are blacks the only people unable to continue living in San Francisco. Families with low or moderate incomes are another. Just between 2002 and 2006, the number of San Francisco households with incomes below $150,000 declined by more than 16,000, while the number of households with incomes of $150,000 and up increased by more than 17,000.

As for children, numerous schools have had to be closed in many coastal California communities, as families with children have been forced out by high housing costs. During Palo Alto's sharp increase in housing prices, school enrollment declined from 15,000 to 9,000, leading to a number of school closings in that community. People young enough to have school-age children have usually not yet reached their peak income earning years, when they might be able to afford high housing prices.

Whatever the vision or the accompanying rhetoric, what people say or even what they intend is far less important than what the actual consequences of their actions are, even if these consequences are ignored by the media and others when those consequences do not fit the prevailing vision. But, however irrelevant rhetoric may be to questions of fact, political rhetoric has played a major role in the creation of housing policies that have been disastrous.

THE RHETORIC OF HOUSING

The verbal packaging of housing policies has been crucial to mobilizing wide political support from people who have no material vested interest in the issues at hand. Land use restrictions, for example, would have far less appeal if called simply "land use restrictions," as they are by scholars specializing in the study of housing. But when verbally packaged as "open space" laws "protecting the environment," or policies "preserving farmland" for future generations, preventing "urban sprawl" or "preserving" places that are "historic," these impediments to building homes take on an idealistic glow that can attract much wider support from people with no such personal stake as might cause them to scrutinize the specifics behind these glowing generalities.

We have already seen some of the economically devastating effects of "open space" laws, for example, especially on the less affluent, minorities and people with school-age children. The economic and social effects of some of the other rhetoric common in discussions of housing issues require similar scrutiny.

"Protecting" and "Saving"

Some of the most powerful political rhetoric is based on undefined words— protecting what is called "our community" or the "fragile" environment, or bumper stickers that simply say "Save Pete's Harbor." Why a particular status quo should be protected or saved— or from whom— are questions seldom investigated and sometimes not even defined. Nor do those who speak constantly of "fragile" environments usually offer any empirically testable definition that would allow anyone to say that environment *A* is fragile and environment *B* is not, or provide any empirical test of whether one is more fragile than the other.

Since the fundamental problem of any economy— whether capitalist, socialist, feudal or whatever— is the allocation of scarce resources which have alternative uses, the fundamental policy issue is why the government should intervene to direct those resources to one citizen rather than another. This is especially so in the United States, where the Constitution decrees "equal protection" to all Americans. Saving Pete's Harbor means denying others the right to use that area for different purposes than those of the status quo. Mere assertions of the superiority of one set of uses over another cannot be decisive because each side can call its preferred uses superior. Nor is there any generally compelling reason why the issue should be settled by rhetorical skills, when the contending interests can put their money where their mouths are, bidding against each other for the use of the same resource, as is done all the time in a market economy. If there is some special reason for exempting Pete's Harbor from this process, then that specific reason is what needs to be heard, rather than rhetoric about "saving" Pete's Harbor.

Some of the most politically powerful rhetoric in defense of housing restrictions have taken the form of claims of saving or protecting "our community." Upscale communities like Loudoun County, Virginia, that keep moderate-income or low-income people from moving in, by such things as requiring several acres of land per house, would never gain public support by saying that they want to keep out the masses to protect the elite. Instead, the argument by such communities is that they are protecting "our community" and its "way of life" or perhaps its natural environment. What all this boils down to is that what they want is to be made legally preemptive over what anybody else wants, the 14th Amendment to the Constitution ("equal protection of the laws") notwithstanding.

Despite the rhetoric, what is called "our community" is in fact *not* their community. Each individual owns only that individual's private property and nobody owns the whole community. Obvious as this might seem, it is easily lost sight of in the rush of heady rhetoric. Sometimes all the land owned by everyone living in the community is only a fraction of the land in or near the community where people are forbidden to build anything.

For example, in Salinas, California, which has had the dubious distinction of having the most unaffordable housing in the nation— with housing costs taking 60 percent of the average income— the amount of land off-limits to building in Monterey County, where Salinas is located, is three times as much as the land actually owned by all the county inhabitants combined. In short, vast amounts of land for which the local inhabitants have paid nothing is nevertheless controlled by them politically for their own benefit, to provide a buffer zone between themselves and less affluent people.

"Nobody wants to give up this way of life," said a local resident with a 16-acre estate. What other people have to give up, in order for her way of life to continue unchanged does not matter, so long as such conflicts of interest are settled politically— in a process in which only those who are there already can vote. Her right to live as she pleases on her 16 acres of land is extended politically to her being able to prevent other people from living as they might choose on vastly more land in the same county, land for which she has paid nothing.

The idea of freezing current land use patterns by law is a radical departure from the history of housing and other land uses in the United States. Harlem was once farmland, far out in the country, and later became an urban middle class Jewish community, before becoming a working class black community. In Los Angeles, cows once grazed on land near what is today U.C.L.A.

The idea of freezing land use patterns in upscale communities, where people want to keep things the way they are, means denying other people the same rights as the existing inhabitants had when they decided where they wanted to live— that is, it denies others the "equal protection of the laws" promised by the 14th Amendment to the Constitution of the United States. To do all of this because the current inhabitants choose to call an area "our community," that does not in fact belong to them, is one sign of the power of political rhetoric. Moreover, this stopping other people from doing what they want to do, so that you can do what you want to do, is considered by many to be an expression of idealism, rather than consummate selfishness.

Sometimes an aura of far-sighted wisdom is projected by claims that things are being preserved for "posterity." But this simply means preserving the same privilege for the posterity of existing residents to keep out the posterity of other people. Often an image is invoked of trying to keep the last few patches of greenery from being paved over— in a country where trees alone cover more than six times the area of all the urban communities put together. Among the other jerry-built rationales for arbitrary restrictions is preserving farmland, without any coherent argument as to why farmland should be frozen in perpetuity, in a country with chronic agricultural surpluses for generations on end.

In short, most of the rhetoric of preservation cannot survive even a modest amount of scrutiny. But, politically, there is no reason why it must. The power of a vision is shown, not by the amount of hard evidence or logical analysis it has, but precisely by the fact that it needs neither of these things to succeed politically. The current economic crisis is just one of the fruits of the political success of rhetoric and visions.

"The Market" versus "Social Programs"

One of the most misleading terms used by people on both sides of many economic and social issues is "the market." This word creates the impression of some kind of impersonal mechanism, when it is as personal as the people in it. The market is nothing more and nothing less than many people competing with one another, and making voluntary transactions with each other, on such terms as are mutually agreeable. Equally misleading is the term "social programs," which has a much softer sound. Who, after all, could be against things that are "social," as distinct from "the dictates of the market"? But such rhetoric turns reality upside down. It is precisely "the market" that is voluntary and "social" programs that mean following government orders.

Decisions made in "the market"— that is, by voluntarily chosen transactions— differ from decisions made by government in fundamental ways that have much to do with how the housing boom was generated. Economic decisions and political decisions are made under very different incentives and constraints.

One of the biggest differences between economic decisions in the market and political decisions in government is that *costs* are an inescapable factor in economic decisions, while political decisions can often ignore costs— especially costs that fall on other people besides the advocates of particular policies or those government officials who impose those policies. That is nowhere more true than in housing markets, where even enormous costs can be — and have been— ignored completely.

A study of housing costs, for example, found that land-use restrictions in the name of "smart-growth" policies had added costs of more than $100,000 per home in 50 metropolitan areas. In a community of just 10,000 families, that adds up to more than a billion dollars' worth of extra housing costs loaded onto the people in such a small community, often on the basis of little more than some fashionable but unexamined phrases about "smart growth," "open space" and the like. That means a billion dollars *less* for maintaining the standard of living of those 10,000 families. In a city of a million families, that means $100 billion subtracted from the standard of living of those who live there. In places like coastal California, the artificial reduction of people's standard of living would be even more.

Crusades for land use restrictions, whether in the name of "open space," "smart growth" or other rationales, are never cast in terms of how many hundreds of thousands of dollars this will add to the price of an average home. Proposals of height restrictions on apartment buildings are never cast in terms of how much higher the rents will have to be when those seeking to build a ten-story building are forced to build two five-story buildings instead, especially in places where the cost of the land greatly exceeds the cost of what is built on the land. Neither the costs of particular requirements imposed by planning commissions nor the costs of the years-long delays that the planning commission approval process can take are calculated or considered. Advocates of such things as "open space" laws or planning commissions usually simply discuss the benefits they anticipate from having these things.

In short, the weighing of benefits against costs, which is common and inescapable in the economic decisions of individuals, families or multinational corporations, is often completely absent in political decisions of government that do not involve any direct expenditures by the government itself, but which can entail billions of dollars in costs in local communities and trillions of dollars when nationwide policies are involved, especially in housing markets.

Many of the decisions made by government agencies overseeing the housing market involve no significant expenditures from the budgets of those agencies, but can entail vast costs and vast risks to others that are seldom even discussed. This is especially so when there is some political crusade for a desirable goal, such as wider home ownership, whose benefits are fervently proclaimed but whose costs and risks receive little or no attention, except for dismissing the arguments of others who try to warn about those costs and risks.

Not only politicians, but social crusaders of various sorts as well, seldom count the costs or weigh the further

repercussions of what they are advocating. Trade-offs do not
make for rousing rhetoric, dramatic placards or catchy
bumper stickers.

It is very doubtful if many in academic communities who
have campaigned zealously for land use restrictions under
any of the heady and lofty labels used for these restrictions,
have any idea that they are in any way responsible for the
dire financial conditions in the country today or for the
hundreds of thousands of workers who have lost their jobs.
Social crusaders are not forced to confront the consequences
of their choices, even in their own minds or consciences,
much less pay a tangible price for the havoc they leave in
their wake while feeling noble.

Chapter 5

The Past and the
Future

A historian once said: "Bad ages to live through are good ages to learn from." The current economic crisis has certainly been a bad time to live through, so we can at least try to learn from it. Indeed, there are many things to *un*-learn from it.

Perhaps the first thing to question is the conclusion that many seem to be deriving from today's economic debacle—namely, that more government regulation of the housing and financial markets could have prevented the housing boom and bust, with its dire repercussions, and more government regulation is the way to prevent a recurrence of today's crisis. We have seen, however, that government regulations and interventions are precisely what pushed lending institutions to reduce the standards which they had traditionally required of prospective borrowers before making mortgage loans to them. This lowering of mortgage loan standards, and the riskier loans that resulted, were crucial to the creation of a whole financial house of cards, whose collapse sent shock waves throughout the American economy, and whose repercussions have been felt internationally.

Those who are saying today that *better* regulation could lead to better results are voicing an attractive truism that is very misleading in the real world. No doubt perfect government regulation could have solved the housing market problems. But a perfect operation of the free market could have solved those problems as well. And perfect human beings could have prevented the problems from arising in the first place. But any serious attempt to deal with serious problems must begin with human beings, and human institutions, as they are— not as we wish or hope they are.

In a complex story about intricate financial arrangements, it is possible to lose sight of a plain and fundamental fact— that behind all the esoteric securities and sophisticated financial dealings are simple, monthly mortgage payments from millions of home buyers across the country. When many of those payments stop coming, no amount of financial expertise in Wall Street or government regulatory intervention from Washington can save the whole investment structure built up on the foundation of those mortgage payments.

The bedrock question then is: Why did so many monthly mortgage payments stop coming? And the bedrock answer is: Because mortgage loans were made to more people whose prospects of repaying them were less than in the past. Nor was this simply a matter of misjudgment by banks and other lenders. The political pressures to meet arbitrary lending quotas, set by officials with the power of economic life and death over banks and over Fannie Mae and Freddie Mac, led to riskier lending practices than in the past.

Human beings make mistakes in both markets and government, despite the widespread notion that, when things go wrong in the market, that automatically means that the government should intervene— as if government makes no mistakes.* But neither sainthood nor infallibility is the norm in Washington or in Wall Street. Any realistic assessment of the decision-making process in the market or in government must examine the incentives and constraints facing those who operate in these two venues. Above all, such an examination must be based on the hard facts about the actual consequences of decisions, regardless of the goals, hopes or rhetoric of those decisions.

POLITICAL INTERVENTIONS

Government actions cannot be discussed as if government is simply the public interest personified. Government actions are political actions, and nowhere more so than in a democracy. The time horizon of elected officials is all too often bounded by the next election. Quick fixes are one result. Nor is this something new or peculiar to American politics. Writing in Britain back in 1776, Adam Smith referred to "that insidious and crafty animal, vulgarly called a statesman or politician, whose councils are directed by the momentary fluctuations of affairs."

Many of the "problems" which politicians set out to "solve," are bad consequences of previous quick-fix "solutions" created by the same politicians or by other politicians. These include housing prices in some places that take half a family's income just to put a roof over their heads. Dealing with this problem by launching nationwide housing crusades to create "affordable housing" through

---

*When a starting quarterback throws an interception, the coach does not immediately take him out of the game and send in a backup quarterback. Decisions in sports are often more rational than decisions in politics because the consequences are immediate and direct, in lost games and fired coaches. No amount of rhetoric or spin can trump what the won and lost columns say.

mortgage lending quotas and riskier lending practices tries to solve one problem by creating another. The collapse of this "solution" now confronts the country with a still bigger problem for which yet a new "solution" is being proposed, with the prospect of still bigger problems for this generation and for generations to come, who will have to pay off a national debt created by politicians who throw around the word "trillion" to the point where it has become familiar enough that its magnitude and dangers no longer evoke the alarm that they once would have.

However easy it may be for politicians to ignore the economic repercussions of their decisions, the costs of such repercussions are virtually inescapable in the marketplace, for they are reflected in prices, even if the individual decision-maker has no clue as to why those prices are what they are. For example, a photographer who wants to buy a telephoto lens, and is choosing between two lenses of the same quality and magnification, may prefer the one that lets in more light. While the photographer may have no idea what additional optical problems are created when a lens is built wider to let in more light, or the more complex lenses made of more expensive glass that may be needed to handle those additional problems, nevertheless the huge price difference between the two lenses conveys all the information needed for decision-making. It is then up to the photographer to decide how much more light is worth how many hundreds more dollars, given the kinds of photographs that the particular photographer takes.

Facts have no such coercive power in politics as they have in markets. While a photographer who knows nothing about optical science is nevertheless forced to confront the fact that a particular lens that lets in more light can cost twice as much as a similar lens without this feature, the situation is completely different in politics, where what most voters believe, or can be induced to believe, is the ultimate reality for elected officials.

Ironically, two economists in the Soviet Union saw a key fact about market economies that so many who live in market economies have missed: "Everything is interconnected in the world of prices, so that the smallest change in one element is passed along the chain to millions of others." In politics, however, "good things" can be advocated or enacted into law on the basis of the beneficial consequences anticipated, with little or no consideration of the many other repercussions that spread in all directions.

Setting an interest-rate ceiling, for example, may be intended to benefit borrowers but it creates incentives for lenders to lend only to people whose prospects of repayment are sufficiently high to make lending profitable at that imposed interest rate. Loan applicants are not "qualified" or "unqualified" absolutely. People whom it would be too risky to lend to at an interest rate of 5 percent may be worth lending to at an interest rate of 10 percent, with the extra interest covering higher rates of default. If an interest rate ceiling imposed by government is lowered enough, it would pay to lend only to millionaires— and, at a still lower interest rate ceiling, it would pay to lend only to billionaires.

However politically attractive interest rate ceilings might be, they make it less likely that lower income people will get loans. And if different racial or ethnic groups are disproportionately represented in lower income brackets, then interest rate ceilings virtually guarantee that they will be disproportionately represented among those turned down for loans, including mortgage loans. For politicians, however, this differential in mortgage loan approvals can then become simply another isolated "problem" in the market for them to "solve"— with no awareness of how previous political "solutions" helped create this situation, much less any consideration of how the repercussions of their own new "solution" will spread in all directions.

Those with a taste for moral melodrama are all too willing to attribute different prices, differing interest rates or other differences to "greed," "racism" or other moral failings of other people. The flaws and shortcomings of human beings virtually guarantee that there will be examples. But examples do not provide an over-all explanation. Moreover, wrong explanations are not just an intellectual problem, when they lead to laws and policies geared to a different situation from that actually existing in the real world.

Another crucial difference between markets and politics is that markets usually leave no choice between changing mistaken notions or paying big-time in lost money or even outright bankruptcy. Under the pressure of such alternatives, the market has already responded quickly to the housing crisis, with a drastic reduction in interest-only loans, no-down-payment loans and other such "creative" financing. But there is no such renunciation of pet notions in Washington. On the contrary, politicians who have played a major role in ruining the housing market are now eager to try their luck intervening in the automobile industry and other sectors of the economy.

Survival in the market often requires recognizing mistakes and changing course, while survival in politics often requires denying mistakes, continuing the current policies and blaming the bad consequences on others. We have already seen in Chapter 4 how impervious to experience government decision-making can be, when the notion of improved housing's beneficial influence on social behavior has persisted for more than a century— and counting— despite such widespread and devastating evidence to the contrary as the degeneration of brand new public housing projects across the country into cesspools of crime, violence and vandalism when slum dwellers moved into these new homes and created new slums.

Despite such massive evidence, Section 8 housing vouchers continue the same notion in a different form, sending dysfunctional people to plague neighborhoods to which many other people have moved, often at some financial sacrifice over a period of years, precisely in order to escape such dysfunctional people. But those who make such government decisions, and those who applaud them from the sidelines, pay no price for persisting in empirically discredited assumptions. Perhaps if Section 8 vouchers were increased in value to the point where they would pay for living in Hollywood, or on Cape Cod, or in affluent gated communities where so many self-congratulatory believers in such social engineering live, then first-hand experience might have some hope of overcoming fashionable notions.

More generally, what is called a "solution" in politics is often simply a patch put over problems caused by previous political "solutions," which in turn were patches put over other political "solutions" before that. What never seems to get through to many politicians, or to supporters of political interventions in markets, is that policies have repercussions far beyond the particular goals of those policies.

In 2000, for example, Hillary Clinton called for tripling the number of Section 8 housing vouchers and building more public housing. In 2007, after the housing bubble burst, Senator Clinton proposed a plan "to preserve the American dream of home ownership" that would "curb unfair lending practices and hold brokers and lenders accountable, give families the support they need to avoid foreclosure and increase the supply of affordable housing." This was the same approach that had led to the housing crisis in the first place, now spiced up with depictions of victims and villains.

To single out home ownership or any other goal as the crusade of the day— as a "good thing"— ignores the fact that virtually nothing is a good thing categorically. We must have food to live but, beyond some point, an increasing intake of food makes us overweight and shortens our lives. Home ownership has undoubted benefits but it also has costs and risks, however much those costs and risks were ignored, downplayed or dismissed by politicians and social crusaders during the housing crusades that led to the boom and bust. As of 2006, a larger proportion of homeowners than of renters were paying more than 50 percent of their incomes for housing.

The disasters into which the heedless political pursuit of ever larger statistics on home ownership has led should at least make us aware of the dangers created by such heady and heedless adventures in the housing markets. An optimist might even hope that it would make us aware of the dangers of heady and heedless adventures in general.

The financial markets that are at the center of our current economic problems have, over the generations, seen one government patch after another put on problems created by previous government patches. Perhaps the crown jewel of those who believe in government intervention in financial markets has been the Federal Deposit Insurance Corporation, which guarantees bank accounts and thus has effectively put an end to runs on banks. There is no question that FDIC, by removing the incentives to start a run on a bank by those fearful of losing the money in their accounts, has reduced bank failures.

But why was such a law necessary in the first place? Because of massive bank failures during the Great Depression of the 1930s. Yet what has seldom been mentioned is that a wholly disproportionate share of those banks that failed then were in states with laws preventing a bank from having more than one location.

Whatever the rationale for preventing banks from having multiple branches, the economic consequence was increased risk. A bank located solely in a wheat-growing community is exposed to all the risks of a fluctuating wheat market, since both its depositors and those to whom it lends money are likely to include many people dependent on the price of wheat, which fluctuates in a world market beyond their control. But a bank with branches not only in wheat-growing areas, but also in steel-producing areas, furniture-making areas, etc., has more diversified risks, and therefore lower risks overall, since all these markets are unlikely to fluctuate the same way at the same time.

It was precisely in states with laws forbidding multiple branches of banks that *state* deposit insurance arose, years before federal deposit insurance. In short, politicians were trying to solve a problem which politicians had created— namely, heightened risks of bank failures. Eventually, Washington politicians put a bigger patch over the patches of state politicians. That it was a good patch is undeniable. But it was solving a problem disproportionately created by other politicians, rather than by the market.

Even during the depths of the Great Depression, when thousands of American banks failed, larger banks with diversified risks, located in places where they were not constrained by state laws against multiple branches, had very low rates of failure. Ninety percent of the failing banks were in small communities and almost all were in states with laws against branch banking. Meanwhile, in Canada, which went through the same depression as the United States, there was *not one bank failure* during the years when thousands of American banks failed— and the Canadian government did not provide deposit insurance.

Canada had 10 banks, with 3,000 branches across the country. The market can work— but only when politicians allow it to work.

No doubt there are things that federal regulatory agencies could have done to keep financial institutions in Wall Street and elsewhere from adding to the risks in an already risky situation by the way they marketed securities based on mortgages. But these are things downstream from the fundamental source of risk, the lowering of standards for making mortgage loans and the resulting delinquencies, defaults and foreclosures.

What an ideal regulatory agency *could* do is no clue whatever to what actual regulatory agencies are *likely* to do, especially with members of Congress like Barney Frank and Christopher Dodd breathing down their necks. What banks could have done ideally in the past or can do ideally in the future is no clue to what they have done or will do when government agencies from the Federal Reserve System to the Justice Department are telling banks that they had better meet arbitrary quotas in their lending if they want to avoid big trouble from the government.

In housing markets, there have been an abundance of theories and of fervently believed doctrines, but not nearly such an abundance of willingness to subject those theories and doctrines to the test of evidence. Politicians would be gambling their entire careers on a roll of the dice, if they were to publicly subject the policies and programs that they have been advocating for years to empirical tests of their consequences. For others outside of politics, their only stake might be ego or ideology, but some people have been known to risk their lives for such things.

Most members of the general public have no such vested interests at risk when deciding whether belief *A* proves to be more consistent with the facts than belief *B*. That is one of the few hopeful aspects of the financial crisis we are in—that there are many people who just want to know what the truth is, so that we can all avoid a repetition of the disaster that has overtaken us, regardless of what theory, doctrine, political party or editorial position is vindicated or discredited in the process.

Consequences

Let us go back to square one to consider the empirical consequences of policies in the housing market. Politicians in Washington set out to solve a national problem *that did not exist*— a nationwide shortage of "affordable housing"—and have now left us with a problem whose existence is as undeniable as it is painful. When the political crusade for affordable housing took off and built up steam during the 1990s, the share of their incomes that Americans were spending on housing in 1998 was 17 percent, compared to 30 percent in the early 1980s. Even during the housing boom of 2005, the median home took just 22 percent of the median American income.

What created the illusion of a nationwide problem was that, in particular localities around the country, housing prices had skyrocketed to the point where people had to pay half their income to buy a modest-sized home and often resorted to very risky ways of financing the purchase. In Tucson, for example, "roughly 60% of first-time home buyers make no down payment and instead now use 100% financing to get into the market," according to the *Wall Street Journal.* Almost invariably, these locally extreme housing prices have been a result of local political crusades in the name of locally attractive slogans about the environment, open space, "smart growth" or whatever other phrases had political resonance at the particular time and place.

Where housing markets have been more or less left alone— in places like Houston or Dallas, for example— housing did not take even half as big a share of family incomes as did comparable housing in places like the San Francisco Bay Area, where heavily hyped political crusades had led to severe restrictions on building. It was in precisely these extremely high housing cost enclaves that the kind of people for whom the national housing crusade expressed much concern— minorities, low-income people and families with children— were forced *out* disproportionately.

Few things blind human beings to the actual consequences of what they are doing like a heady feeling of self-righteousness during a crusade to smite the wicked and rescue the downtrodden. Statistical studies about disparities between blacks and whites in mortgage loan approval rates might be said to have "jump-started" the housing crusades that began in the 1990s. Politicians and the media led this crusade, with many community activists following in their wake, much like scavengers, able to extract large sums of money from banks and other institutions by raising claims of discrimination, whose power to delay government approval of bank mergers and other business decisions made pay-offs to these activists the only prudent course for those accused.

Even where loudly proclaimed concern for the poor and minorities gave impetus to the drive for over-riding traditional mortgage lending standards, this is not to say that the poor and minorities were the sole beneficiaries or even the main beneficiaries. When you open the floodgates, you cannot tell the water where to go. Housing speculators— "flippers"— found the new and looser home mortgage rules a bonanza. So did many others. It is by no means clear that the poor or minorities came out ahead at all, after the housing boom turned to bust and many were left with mortgage payments they couldn't meet on homes they couldn't afford.

With rich rewards available— politically, ideologically and financially— from the "affordable housing" crusade, there were ample incentives to keep this crusade going for years. Meanwhile, various special interests found ways to benefit themselves from all this, whether as home builders, real estate investors or others, and therefore added their voices in support of the open-ended goal of more home ownership through various ways of achieving, or seeming to achieve, affordable housing. Supporters of such policies and programs easily drowned out the voices of those economists and others who increasingly warned of the risky financial arrangements that were behind the statistics on the growing numbers of home buyers that were so triumphantly being paraded as fruits of the crusade for affordable housing and the stamping out of mortgage lending discrimination.

In short, this was a crusade that was feeding on its own successes by its own criteria, and was not likely to stop unless it got stopped.

The housing market collapse dealt a blow to some of the devices that fed the crusade— "creative" financing and lax lending standards, for example— but even the ensuing national crisis did nothing to end the political attractiveness of the goal of making housing affordable by government fiat, rather than by individuals buying or renting housing that was within their own income range. Just as the utter discrediting of public housing projects did not discredit the underlying beliefs that caused such projects to be built, so in this case even the more widely disastrous consequences of the affordable housing crusade have led only to seeking other ways of carrying on that same crusade, based on the same discredited assumptions and the same disregard of repercussions.

While some Congressional Democrats have proposed a moratorium on mortgage foreclosures or allowing judges to change the terms of mortgage contracts, Senate Republicans have proposed "providing government-backed, 4% fixed mortgages to any credit-worthy borrower." What these proposals from politicians of both parties all have in common is an utter absence of any serious consideration of the repercussions in multiple directions of arbitrary government fiats.

Anyone who expected any such consideration of repercussions by most members of either political party would have little chance of avoiding painful disappointments. Certainly few politicians of either party have questioned whether the track record of politicians in the housing market justified more of the same in other markets. Many are in fact eager to extend political intervention into other industries receiving the government "stimulus" or bailout money.

THE NEW DEAL IDEAL

Whatever the long-run prospects for more rational government policies in the future, the current disaster is already upon us, and how it is dealt with by those in power is the pressing issue of the day.

Many of the policies for dealing with the current financial crisis are reminiscent of the policies of Franklin D. Roosevelt's New Deal administration for dealing with the Great Depression of the 1930s. Indeed, many of the advocates of such policies today cite the New Deal as a model for government intervention to bring the economy out of an economic crisis. Congressman Barney Frank, for example, said, "This is equivalent to what FDR had to do. . .to save capitalism from its own excesses." A front-page *Los Angeles Times* column was titled "A Time for Boldness Beyond the New Deal," and claimed that the New Deal "wasn't stimulative enough." But, before using the New Deal as a model, we should examine that history more carefully than many have done.

The Stock Market Crash

The huge stock market crash of 1929 has long been regarded as the cause of the massive unemployment that marked the decade of the 1930s. The tragedy of that decade is undeniable. Not only did unemployment soar as high as 25 percent for 1933, the annual unemployment rate remained above 20 percent for four consecutive years, 1932 through 1935. Literally thousands of banks failed across the country. Stock prices fell to a fraction of their 1929 peaks, as American corporations as a whole operated in the red for two consecutive years. Mass foreclosures of homes and farms drove families into makeshift housing, including shanty towns christened "Hoovervilles" for President Herbert Hoover, who was widely blamed for this catastrophe that struck while he was in the White House.

The view that Hoover's successor, Franklin D. Roosevelt, was responsible for getting the country out of the Great Depression was once widespread and still has enough support among opinion-makers today that a new administration in Washington in 2009 invokes FDR and his policies as a precedent to follow in dealing with today's financial crises. More fundamentally, the Great Depression has been seen— then and now— as a failure of the free market that required massive government intervention to save the economy. FDR has been credited with being the first President of the United States to understand the need for federal intervention to deal with a depression.

This picture, however, has been increasingly challenged in recent years by scholars, especially economists, but also by some historians as well.

While federal intervention in the economy during the Great Depression was indeed on an unprecedented scale, it is now increasingly recognized that this intervention was begun by President Herbert Hoover, and that Franklin D. Roosevelt's New Deal was largely a further expansion of what Hoover had already begun. Even at the time, Walter Lippmann pointed this out in a 1935 newspaper column:

> The policy initiated by President Hoover in the autumn of 1929 was something utterly unprecedented in American history. The national government undertook to make the whole economic order operate prosperously. . . . the Roosevelt measures are a continuous evolution of the Hoover measures.

President Hoover was himself well aware that he was doing something unprecedented by intervening in the economy to try to get the country out of a depression. "No President before had ever believed there was a government responsibility in such cases," he said in his memoirs. Even former members of President Franklin D. Roosevelt's own administration admitted in later years that many of Hoover's initiatives were taken over and expanded under FDR, though the political and media image of Hoover invoked in many election years thereafter was that Hoover had been a "do nothing president."

The real question, however, is not who should be credited with first taking on the responsibility for initiating federal intervention, but whether that intervention itself deserves credit, in the first place. Today it is so widely accepted that the federal government must "do something" to cope with recessions and depressions that the actual consequences of government interventions tend to receive relatively little scrutiny in the media or in politics.

Job Creation

Since mass unemployment was the most visibly painful aspect of the Great Depression, one of the main thrusts of the Roosevelt administration then, like that of the Obama administration today, was to create jobs.

During the Great Depression of the 1930s, the government created vast numbers of jobs— there were more young men in the Civilian Conservation Corps than in the Army— but unemployment never fell below double digits during the first seven years under President Franklin D. Roosevelt. For the first 21 consecutive months of FDR's administration, unemployment never fell below 20 percent. The fallacy of those who see government-created jobs as an answer to unemployment is in regarding such jobs as a *net increase* in employment. But the money that pays for government-created jobs is taken from the private sector, leaving less demand and less employment there. Huge increases in government-created jobs may make little or no net difference in mass unemployment.

There are ways in which government policies can, theoretically, create a net increase in employment. But this is a little like saying that better regulation can prevent crises in financial markets. It is true in the abstract but the real question in the real world is whether what government is likely to do is likely to increase employment on net balance. The track record of the New Deal offers little support to that conclusion.

Whatever its shortcomings economically, what government job creation programs can do politically is create a large class of people beholden to the government and likely to vote for those who gave them jobs in hard times. The *political* success of the New Deal is beyond dispute. That FDR could be re-elected in a landslide in 1936 and re-elected again to an unprecedented third term in 1940, despite never having gotten unemployment down into single digits during his first two terms, is a sign that President Obama may also be able to succeed politically, even if his policies turn out to be an economic disaster for the country as a whole.

Market versus Government

The larger question that remains as relevant as ever today is: Was it the failure of the free market that led to the massive unemployment which persisted throughout the decade of the 1930s or was the Great Depression prolonged by the government interventions that were intended to shorten it?

Two facts are clear from the outset: (1) the stock market crash in October 1929 marked a major downturn in the economy as a whole and a rise in unemployment; and (2) during all the previous history of the United States, when the federal government let the economy recover from downturns on its own, no depression was ever as deep or as long-lasting as the Great Depression of the 1930s. In short, a plausible case can be made that either the market or the government was responsible for the severity and duration of the Great Depression. What must be done is to go beyond plausibility and scrutinize the facts more closely.

Because the stock market crash occurred first and the government began to intervene on a large scale some time later, we can trace what happened before and after the federal interventions, which began under Herbert Hoover and continued under Franklin D. Roosevelt. Month by month statistics on unemployment, compiled in the late twentieth century by economists Richard Vedder and Lowell Gallaway, enable us to follow events in some detail.

Two months after the stock market crash in October 1929, unemployment rose and peaked at 9 percent, after which it began a generally downward movement over the next several months and subsided to a level of 6.3 percent by June 1930. Although these levels of unemployment were higher than those before the stock market crash, and were a legitimate cause for concern, they were not even half of the unemployment rate that would begin, and persist for years, after major federal interventions in the economy.

The first of these major interventions began in June 1930, when Congress passed the Smoot-Hawley tariffs, the highest in more than a century, in an effort to reduce imports and thus preserve American jobs by having the formerly imported goods produced in the United States instead. As already noted, unemployment stood at 6.3 percent at this time. In November of 1930, unemployment reached double digits for the first time in the decade, at 11.6 percent.

In other words, unemployment had not yet reached double digits until more than a year after the stock market crash. But it reached double digits five months after the Smoot-Hawley tariffs that were supposed to reduce unemployment. Moreover, while the initial rise in unemployment after the stock market crash began to subside after peaking two months later, the double digit unemployment that began after the Smoot-Hawley tariffs continued for every month throughout the entire remainder of the decade of the 1930s.

Not all of this was due to the Smoot-Hawley tariffs alone. These tariffs, passed during the Hoover administration, were only the first in a series of major federal interventions in the market that continued under FDR throughout the remainder of the decade. The biggest of the New Deal interventions was the National Industrial Recovery Act of 1933, which controlled prices and wages in industry. The Agricultural Adjustment Act of 1933 established federal control over prices and output in agriculture. The National Labor Relations Act of 1935 made it mandatory for employers to negotiate wages and working conditions with labor unions. FDR also took the country off the gold standard and issued thousands of executive orders— more than all the subsequent Presidents of the United States in the twentieth century combined.

The New Deal administration not only set up *policies* to deal with existing economic problems of the 1930s, it set up enduring *institutions* to change the way the American economy operated. Thus we are, in the twenty-first century, paying agricultural subsidies to millionaires and billionaires because of a program created during the Great Depression to help small farmers who were having a hard time. Again, once you have opened the floodgates you cannot tell the water where to go. Programs set up to help one constituency acquire new constituencies and take new directions.

The Roosevelt administration's rapid succession of sweeping and unpredictable interventions in the economy, interspersed with anti-business rhetoric, caused even a liberal like John Maynard Keynes to question whether some of the New Deal reforms, including some he regarded as "wise and necessary," might "impede" economic recovery because they could "upset the confidence of the business world and weaken their existing motives to action."

Business investments in fact remained unusually low during the uncertainties of the New Deal era, as investments have tended to remain low during other periods of uncertainty, such as today. According to a financial historian, throughout the 1930s "the amount banks lent for each dollar

of reserves remained at about half the level of the 1920s."
Meanwhile the unemployment rate never fell below the
double-digit level for any year in either of FDR's first two
terms in office. Whatever the vision, that is the record. An
economic and statistical analysis in a leading scholarly journal
concluded that government policies in the 1930s prolonged the
depression by several years.

Ending the Depression

What brought the Great Depression of the 1930s to an
end? Over the years, fewer and fewer people have accepted
the once common belief that it was the New Deal policies of
President Roosevelt that ended the Great Depression. A
competing explanation is that World War II ended the Great
Depression. It is certainly true that unemployment virtually
disappeared during the war and production increased. But
to say that the war ended the depression still leaves
unanswered the real question: What specifically about the
war caused unemployment to fall and output to rise?

Advocates of a massive government spending program
today— the so-called "stimulus package"— argue that it was
the rise of federal spending during the war which supplied
the demand for output and for the labor that produced that
output. This explanation certainly sounds plausible. But the
question is: Are we prepared to bet literally trillions of
dollars in government expenditures today on plausibility,
without bothering to scrutinize that plausible explanation of
what happened when similar policies were tried before?

The mere existence of World War II, which began in
September 1939, did not greatly change output or
employment in the United States, which did not enter the
war until December of 1941. Although the war started in
1939, the unemployment rate in the United States was 14.6

percent in 1940, compared to 14.3 percent three years earlier. So the existence of the war, as such, was clearly not sufficient to end the Great Depression. The first year after 1930 for which the unemployment rate was no longer in double digits was 1941, when unemployment fell to 9.9 percent. High as that might seem today, more than a decade had passed before the unemployment rate dropped even slightly below 10 percent for even a single month. The next year— the first full year when the United States was at war— the unemployment rate fell below 5 percent, and for the next three years it was below two percent.

Clearly the war seems to have had a dramatic effect in reducing unemployment. But the real question still remains: Was that because of federal spending?

As already noted, the unemployment rate in 1940 was 14.6 percent. But the federal deficit was higher in 1936, when the unemployment rate was also higher, at 17 percent. If federal deficit spending is considered to be the crucial factor, then the question must be faced: Why did a bigger deficit not reduce unemployment at the earlier time (1936) compared to the later time (1940)?

President Franklin D. Roosevelt himself put his finger on a change that is today often overlooked by those who attribute the end of the Great Depression to increased government spending during wartime. In his whimsical way that some found charming, FDR said that "Dr. New Deal" was replaced by "Dr. Win-the-War." The Roosevelt administration abandoned its anti-business stance and the pendulum swung to the other side, with cost-plus government contracts that *guaranteed* business profits to producers of war materiel. Taking 12 million men out of the workforce to serve in the military forces also greatly reduced the potential for unemployment, though that aspect is often overlooked by those eager to credit federal spending for ending mass unemployment.

In short, the war ended the New Deal— and the end of the New Deal saw the economy recover, as it had recovered from depressions on its own throughout the history of the country prior to the 1930s.

The Lessons of the New Deal

If there is a lesson in the New Deal experience, it seems to be the opposite of the one drawn by those who have advocated massive government spending and massive government interventions in the economy. The lesson that seems more consistent with the evidence is that massive and unpredictable government interventions in the economy create uncertainties as to what government is going to do next— as well as uncertainties as to what the actual economic consequences of government policies will turn out to be.

In that atmosphere of uncertainty generated by unpredictable government policy experiments, people tend to hold on to their money. The velocity of circulation of money slowed down during the Great Depression, just as it has today. Massive government deficit spending did not stimulate private spending then, any more then than it is stimulating it now.

It is of course not possible to conduct laboratory experiments to determine what would have happened without government intervention after the stock market crash of 1929. The closest thing to such an experiment might be the experience after the stock market crash of 1987, a decline very similar to that in 1929. Unlike what had been done by Presidents Hoover and Roosevelt, however, President Ronald Reagan did *not* intervene in 1987, despite media criticisms of his inaction. The net result of leaving the stock market and the economy to recover on their own was what the distinguished British magazine *The Economist* later called 20 years of "an enviable combination of steady growth and low inflation."

This was not the only time when doing nothing produced a better track record than massive government interventions. Two sharp downturns in the early 1920s were allowed to recover on their own and quickly did so. There have been similar results in other countries. J.A. Schumpeter, writing in the 1930s about an economic downturn in England back in the 1820s, said, "the inaction of government, however reprehensible on humanitarian grounds, contributed to recovery at least by not hampering it." Conservatives have no monopoly on skepticism about government intervention during an economic downturn. It was none other than Karl Marx who referred to "crackbrained meddling by the authorities" that can "aggravate an existing crisis."

Purpose and Success

No one can pronounce the New Deal administration— or today's administration in Washington— either a success or a failure, without knowing what it has been trying to do. What we may wish any administration would be trying to do is no clue to what its actual goals and priorities might be. Nor can we assume that any administration's rhetoric is a reliable guide to its purposes, much less its actual consequences.

Our assessment of the success or failure of the New Deal will be quite different if we assume that its efforts were directed primarily toward getting the country out of the Great Depression as quickly and as fully as possible, rather than some other goal. Walter Lippmann, perhaps the leading journalist of that era, saw the New Deal's primary goal as entirely different from economic recovery.

According to Lippmann, the New Dealers would "rather not have recovery if the revival of private initiative means a resumption of private control in the management of corporate business." He saw their goal as fundamental and enduring changes in the institutions of American society, rather than the most expeditious ending of the current economic crisis. To Lippmann "the essence of the New Deal is the reduction of private corporate control by collective bargaining and labor legislation, on the one side, and by restrictive, competitive and deterrent government action on the other side."

It is a matter of record that many of the leading decision-makers of the New Deal administration in the 1930s were advocates of government intervention in the economy and of a fundamental restructuring of the economy— a New Deal— years *before* the stock market crash of 1929 and the Great Depression that followed, which put them in a position to carry out ideas to which they were dedicated long before there was any economic crisis to deal with. The New Deal succeeded in using a transient crisis to create enduring institutions, including among others the Federal National Mortgage Association or "Fannie Mae," which FDR created in 1938, and which has been at the heart of the housing boom and bust that led to today's financial crises.

What of the new administration of our time? Do its early initiatives indicate that their primary goal is to put the current economic crisis behind us, as quickly and as fully as possible, or *to use that crisis to impose new and enduring changes in the American economy and society?* The answer to that question depends far more on what this administration has actually done, rather than on what it has said.

Within a month after the Obama administration took office in January 2009, a spending bill involving hundreds of billions of dollars was passed in just two days, even though it was more than a thousand pages long and it was virtually impossible that members of Congress could have read it all in the time available.

As noted at the end of Chapter 3, both the Congressional Budget Office in the United States and *The Economist* magazine in Britain pointed out that most of the money in the "stimulus" bill would not be spent in 2009 nor all of it before the end of 2010. Even a supporter of the "stimulus" bill like Professor Alan Blinder of Princeton said, "it's still too slow."

If the purpose was to get the current economic crisis behind us, then the slow-moving policies passed in haste make no sense. But if the purpose is to use the current crisis to create enduring changes in the institutions of the American economy and society, then the haste makes perfect sense. In this latter case, it doesn't matter how slowly the spending gets underway; what matters is how fast the law gets passed, while the public is panicked, and before any opposition can get organized. The massive spending already provided by the Bush administration bailout has provided a basis on which Washington politicians can tell General Motors how to make cars and other companies what their CEOs' salaries should be.

The argument that government officials have a right to protect the taxpayers' money through intervention into the decisions made by companies that spend bailout money is politically effective, however logically deficient. *Rights are not the issue.* Anyone who owns a home has a right to take a hammer and smash every window in that house. But no one believes that the right to do so says anything about the wisdom of doing so. All of us have rights to do all sorts of things that would be counterproductive and even disastrous. The purpose of government is not to exercise every conceivable right it has but to exercise whatever wisdom it has for the benefit of the country.

The current economic crisis itself grew out of politicians intervening in businesses and markets, making decisions for which they have neither experience nor expertise, much less a stake. To extend the same principle to other sectors of the economy is to invite a wider disaster, rather than an end to the current crisis. Asserting a right to do so is completely beside the point— which is whether the country will be better off or worse off if politicians continue the pattern of interventions that brought on the current economic problems in the first place.

Shortly before the Obama administration took office, the man who would become President Obama's chief of staff, Rahm Emanuel, said, "You never want a serious crisis to go to waste." He added: "What I mean by that is that it's an opportunity to do things you could not do before." In other words, both this statement and the deeds of the new administration point toward their using the current crisis to forward their long-run agenda of a politically guided economy. Rushing through legislation toward that end, in the name of ending the crisis, and doing so during the early "honeymoon" period of a new administration, when both the public and the media are uncritical, makes perfect sense in pursuit of such a goal, though it makes little or no sense on an assumption that they are trying to get the economic crisis over as quickly as possible.

Instead, what we are talking about is *using* a crisis to fundamentally and enduringly change the institutions of American society. However confident or enthusiastic the new administration may be about remaking the institutions of America to fit their vision, those institutions have had a remarkably successful track record over a period of more than two centuries. What is now being proposed is to jettison all that for the sake of untried theories, because of an economic situation that has arisen in a relatively few years, as a result of government interventions with a terrible track record that have led to a crisis which now provides an opportunity for more of the same— in the name of "change."

To those who are eager for an expansion of government, the market has always failed. Yet, as an economist at a leading financial firm put it plainly: "Lending money to American homebuyers had been one of the least risky and most profitable businesses a bank could engage in for nearly a century." It was the massive intervention of politicians in the housing market that changed that disastrously, not only for banks but for the entire economy. It is precisely such politicians— indeed, many of the very same individual politicians— who are now seeking to do an encore in other industries. For example, a growing list of government directives are being imposed on banks receiving bailout money:

> Financial institutions that are getting government bailout funds have been told to put off evictions and modify mortgages for distressed homeowners. They must let shareholders vote on executive pay packages. They must slash dividends, cancel employee training and morale-building exercises, and withdraw job offers to foreign citizens.

Whatever the merits or demerits of any of these directives individually, all of them represent things which the Constitution of the United States never authorized the government to do. Moreover, all are things imposed *after* the bailout, not as a precondition for receiving the bailout, and so leave open how many more arbitrary directives will follow. This adds to the uncertainties that inhibit economic activity.

The market has already demonstrated how fast it can adjust to the housing market collapse, when no-down-payment mortgages, interest-only mortgages and other "creative" ways of financing home purchases drastically declined in California, in just a couple of years. But the political arena still abounds with the same vision of government micro-management— and even the same personalities— that put the housing market, and ultimately the economy, on the road to ruin.

Despite differences of personalities and of the times, the underlying vision of the New Deal and that of the current administration are fundamentally similar. However that vision is conceived or articulated by those who believe in it, it is a vision of the federal government exercising vastly more power over the economy and the society than was ever granted to it by the Constitution of the United States. What the government buys with the enormous sums of money it dispenses is the power to give orders to the recipients that the Constitution never authorized them to give. Politicians are, in effect, buying up our freedom with our own tax money.

SUMMARY AND IMPLICATIONS

Before we go forward as a nation, it is well to look at where we have been, despite being urged to take drastic actions immediately— and, in fact, *especially* when being urged to take drastic actions immediately.

Whether we look at the American economy in general or the housing market in particular, we see a history of remarkable progress for generation after generation— and a few recent years when things turned very bad, very quickly.

It has been almost axiomatic, for at least a century, that the American economy produces more output than any other economy in the world. All this is so much taken for granted that no one considers it worth commenting on the fact that 300 million Americans today produce more output than more than a billion people in India or an even larger population in China— indeed, more than these two countries which, put together, have more than eight times the population of the United States. We also produce more than Japan, Germany, Britain and France combined.

The housing market has, of course, changed drastically in the past few years, as have other things in the economy. But does all this suggest that (1) we need to change some recent bad policies or that (2) we need to restructure a whole economic system that has worked well for centuries? More specifically, does it mean that we need to allow politicians a bigger say in how American businesses are run?

Lenders did not spontaneously begin to lend to people who would not have qualified for loans under the traditional criteria that had evolved out of years of experience in the market. Such risky loans were made under growing pressures from government regulatory agencies and politicians, and even threats of prosecution from the Justice Department if the statistical profiles of borrowers whose loan applications were approved did not match the government's preconceptions.

The growth in subprime loans was one way of meeting arbitrary quotas for lending to people who did not meet the criteria for loan approval that had prevailed for years. Quota lending was one of many political patches put over problems caused by previous political "solutions." Often these interventions have focussed on some limited goal, with no real concern about, or even awareness of, the wider ramifications of what they were doing. It is doubtful whether most of the state politicians of the past who enacted laws to prevent branch banking had anything in mind more far-reaching than enabling local banks to avoid having to compete with branches of much bigger and better-known banks. It seems even less likely that these local politicians felt any responsibility for the thousands of bank failures during the Great Depression of the 1930s.

Nor is it likely that the national politicians of our own times, who for years made "home ownership" the touchstone of housing policy, will acknowledge any responsibility for the financial disasters and widespread unemployment today. What that means is that the voting public must at a minimum be skeptical of political spin, no matter how often it is echoed in the media. What would be even better would be to develop some sense of awareness that everything "is interconnected in the world of prices, so that the smallest change in one element is passed along the chain to millions of others." It is a caution especially apt when someone is pushing the political crusade of the day as an overriding "good thing," whether home ownership, mortgage foreclosure mitigation or a restructuring of the whole economy.

The very idea that the current economic crisis will go to "waste" if it is not used by politicians to rush through a fundamental restructuring of the economy, while the public is too panicked to object, should at the very least give us pause, if not set off alarm bells. From the standpoint of those who seek to remake the economic institutions of America, the worst case scenario would be to have the economy begin visibly recovering on its own before they can get their blueprint for salvation enacted into law. The urgency behind the hasty passage of the "stimulus" legislation was real, even if the reason for that haste was not a swift economic recovery.

Will the history of the New Deal and the Great Depression repeat itself? There is, of course, no way to know in advance. However, history has repeated itself many times before, when past experience has been ignored— and especially when past mistakes have been repeated, often in the name of doing something new and different. Comments made years ago by distinguished British historian Paul Johnson remain very apt in our times:

> The study of history is a powerful antidote to contemporary arrogance. It is humbling to discover how many of our glib assumptions, which seem to us novel and plausible, have been tested before, not once but many times and in innumerable guises; and discovered to be, at great human cost, wholly false.

SOURCES

CHAPTER 1: The Economics of the Housing Boom

The increase in the median price of American single-family homes from 2000-2005 is shown on page 162 of the *Financial Services Fact Book, 2007*, published by the Insurance Information Institute. The sharp home price increases in New York, Los Angeles and San Diego are from page 40 of the October 16, 2006 issue of *Newsweek*, in a column titled "The Worrying Housing Bust." That more than two-thirds of mortgage loans originated in 2004 were sold to the secondary market, and that Fannie Mae and Freddie Mac purchased more than a third of such loans was reported on page 355 of the Summer 2005 issue of the *Federal Reserve Bulletin*, under the title "New Information Reported under HMDA and Its Application in Fair Lending Enforcement." The quote about the profits and risks of government-sponsored enterprises is from page A10 of the July 12–13, 2008 issue of the *Wall Street Journal*, under the headline "Fannie Mae Ugly." The fact that home equity accounts for 42% of a household's net worth is from page 4 of "Net Worth and the Assets of Households: 2002," *Current Population Reports*, P70–115, published by the U.S. Census Bureau in April 2008. The statement that mortgage debt represents 82% of a homeowner's liabilities is from page 423 of the October 2003 issue of the *Federal Reserve Bulletin*, under the title "Recent Changes to a Measure of U.S. Household Debt Service." That 60% of a homeowner's income was required to pay the monthly mortgage in Salinas, California, was shown on a graph on page A6 of the August 26–27, 2006 issue of the *Wall Street Journal*, in a front-page story titled "In Tony Monterey County, Slums and a Land War." Changes in the interest rate on a conventional 30-year mortgage from 1973–2005 were shown on page 7 of the October 2006 issue of the *Monthly Labor Review*, in an article titled "Recent Employment Trends in Residential and Nonresidential Construction." That borrowers with higher interest rates tend to have higher rates of payment delinquency and foreclosure was shown on page 368 of the Summer 2005 issue of the *Federal Reserve Bulletin*, under the title "New Information Reported under HMDA and Its Application in Fair Lending Enforcement." The increased reliance on savings as the primary source of a down payment on a home among California home buyers after the housing bust is from page 24 of the report *State of the California Housing Market 2008–2009*, published by the California Association of Realtors. The decreasing proportion of first-time home buyers in California in the early years of the twenty-first century is from page 13 of the same study, while the disparity in the size of down payments between first-time home buyers and repeat home buyers in California is from page 39. The fact that the top ten areas with the highest rates of home price appreciation were in California is from page 4 of the study "California's Newest Homeowners: Affording the Unaffordable," *California Counts: Population Trends and Profiles*, published by the Public Policy Institute of California in August 2005. The increase in home prices in California after the decade of the 1970s is discussed on pages 232–234 of *Regulatory Takings: Law, Economics, and Politics*, by William A. Fischel. The statement that in 2005 the median-priced San Francisco Bay Area home cost more than three times the national average is from page A11 of a front-page story from the October 16, 2005 issue of the *San Francisco Chronicle*, under the headline "Making Ends Meet: Struggling in Middle Class." The fact that the median sales price of a home in San Francisco reached $765,000 in 2005 was reported on page 3 of the study "California's Newest Homeowners: Affording the Unaffordable," *California Counts: Population Trends and Profiles*, published by the Public Policy Institute of California. The $2,000 per day increase in the value of homes in San Mateo County, California, during March 2005 is from page 1 of the April 15, 2005 issue of the *San Mateo County Times*, under the headline "County's Home Prices Bust Record." The statement that the median price for homes in San Mateo County, California, soared to over one million dollars in 2007 is from page 1 of the August 16, 2007 issue of the *San Mateo County Times*, in an article titled "Median Home Cost over $1M," while the relatively small size of these homes is mentioned on page 6 of the same article. That the median sales price for homes in the state of California reached $561,000 in 2006 was shown on page 63 of the study *State of the California Housing Market 2008–2009*, published by the California Association of Realtors. The 13 percent increase nationwide in home price appreciation from 2004–2005, and the rates of appreciation for Arizona and Michigan were reported on pages 1–2 and 15–16 of the report "House Price Appreciation Continues at Robust Pace," published by the Office of Federal Housing Enterprise Oversight on March 1, 2006. The quote about a graduate student in San Francisco "visiting one exorbitantly priced hovel after another" is from page F1 of the September 16, 2007 issue of the *San Francisco Chronicle*, under the headline "Squeeze Hits Landlords." The fact that incomes were rising less rapidly in California than in the rest of the nation at the same time that the state's home prices were soaring is from page 238 of *Regulatory Takings: Law, Economics, and Politics*, by William A. Fischel. The rate of population increase in the San Francisco Bay Area during the 1970s compared with the national rate is from page 9 of a 1982 study by the Stanford Environmental Law Society titled *Land Use and Housing on the San Francisco Peninsula*, edited by Thomas M. Hagler, while the nearly four-fold rise of home prices in Palo Alto, California, during the 1970s when the city's population declined by 8 percent was mentioned on pages 85 and 89. The wide range in the cost of a quarter-acre lot in Chicago, San Diego, New York and San Francisco was noted on pages 15–16 of the study "The Impact of Zoning on Housing Affordability," Working Paper 8835, written by Edward L. Glaeser and Joseph Gyourko and published by the National Bureau of Economic Research in March 2002. The amount of open space in San Mateo County, California, is noted on page 2 of the December 10, 2003 issue of the *San Mateo County Times*, under the headline "Open Space." The connection between home price increases and restrictive land use laws is quoted from page 35 of the study "The Planning Penalty: How Smart Growth Makes Housing Unaffordable," written by Randal O'Toole and published by the Independent Institute in 2006. The fact that 23 of the 26 "severely unaffordable" international urban areas follow "smart-growth" policies is from page 38 of the same study. The quote from the former governor of the Reserve Bank of New Zealand is from the "Introduction" to the study *4th Annual Demographia International Housing Affordability Survey: 2008*. The minimum lot size restrictions enacted in Loudoun County, Virginia, were described on pages B1 and B4 of the July 24, 2001 issue of the *Washington Post*, in an article titled "Loudoun Adopts Strict Controls on Development," while similar restrictions enacted in Fayette County, Kentucky, were mentioned on page 33 of the study, "The Planning Penalty: How Smart Growth Makes Housing Unaffordable," written by Randal O'Toole and published by the Independent Institute in 2006. The wide range in home prices between communities with and without growth-management policies is quoted from page 6 of the same study. The comparison of home prices between Houston and San Jose is from page 8 of the October 17, 2007 issue of *Policy Analysis*, No. 602, in a study titled "Do You Know the Way to L.A.?: San Jose Shows How to Turn an Urban Area into Los Angeles in Three Stressful Decades." The fact that the city of Houston experienced rising income during the 1970s while still maintaining housing affordability is noted on page 32 of "The

Planning Penalty: How Smart Growth Makes Housing Unaffordable," written by Randal O'Toole and published by the Independent Institute in 2006, while the high income and low housing costs in Dallas are mentioned on page 33. The "skyrocketing prices" in Manhattan and the less than 10% increase in the housing stock there from 1980–2005 were noted on pages 332–333 of the October 2005 issue of the *Journal of Law and Economics*, under the title "Why Is Manhattan So Expensive?: Regulation and the Rise in Housing Prices." The almost tripling of the population of the city of Las Vegas between 1980–2000 at a time when the real median home price remained unchanged was mentioned on page 332 of the same study. The rise in Las Vegas home prices in recent years as a result of the increased resistance of environmental groups to land development was discussed on page 125 of *The Best-Laid Plans* by Randal O'Toole. Information on the extent of development of the land area of the United States is from page 143 of *Sprawl: A Compact History* by Robert Bruegmann and pages 56–57 of *The Road More Traveled* by Ted Balaker and Sam Staley. Congressman Dick Armey's quote is from page 183 of his book *Armey's Axioms*. The increased affordability of housing in most of the nation in 2005 was reported on page A1 of the December 29, 2005 issue of the *New York Times*, under the headline "Twenty Years Later, Buying a House Is Less of a Bite." That housing costs in the ten most expensive metropolitan areas were more than twice the national average in 2004 is from page A1 of the September 22, 2004 issue of the *Wall Street Journal*, in an article titled "After Big Run-Up in Real Estate, Some on Coasts Are Cashing Out." The disparity in the share of income required to pay housing costs in high-priced cities like New York and Los Angeles compared to affordable communities such as Tampa and Dallas was reported on pages A1 and C9 of the December 29, 2005 issue of the *New York Times*, under the headline "Twenty Years Later, Buying a House Is Less of a Bite." That creative mortgage products such as interest-only loans and adjustable-rate mortgages kept initial monthly mortgage payments down in the early years of the twenty-first century was reported on page D1 of the July 14, 2005 issue of the *Wall Street Journal*, under the headline "Housing Gets Even Less Affordable." Data on the growth of interest-only mortgage loans from 2002–2005 are from page A16 of the May 20, 2005 issue of the *San Francisco Chronicle*, in a front-page story titled "High Interest in Interest-Only Home Loans," and also from pages C1 and C6 of the July 15, 2006 issue of the *New York Times*, in an article titled "Keep Eyes Fixed on Variable Mortgages."

The Chicago man who took out a home equity loan on his home, which had vastly appreciated in price, was mentioned on page 18 of the June 13, 2005 issue of *Time*, under the headline "America's House Party." The story of the Oakland family who refinanced and ultimately lost their home to foreclosure was told on pages A1 and A21 of the August 10, 2008 issue of the *San Francisco Chronicle*, under the headline "Foreclosed Family's Last Goodbye to Home." The soaring value of home equity loans from 2003–2007 was noted on page 165 of the *Financial Services Fact Book, 2009*, published by the Insurance Information Institute. The increase in the use of "cash-out refinancing" by homeowners during the housing boom was reported on page 167 of the same study and also page 26 of the February 2009 issue of *The American Spectator*, in an article titled "The True Origins of This Financial Crisis." The rise in reverse mortgages from 2001–2005 was shown on page 156 of the *Financial Services Fact Book, 2007*, published by the Insurance Information Institute. The decrease in homeowners' equity as a share of home value from 1945 to 2003 is from page 55 of the April 19, 2004 issue of *Newsweek*, in a column titled "Is Housing a New Bubble?" Accounts of speculators making large profits by "flipping" houses are from page 83 of the April 2005 issue of *Money*, under the headline "They Call Them Flippers," and also from page 71 of the October 3, 2005 issue of *Forbes*, in an article titled "Diamonds in the Rough." The statement that nearly 15% of adjustable rate mortgages had initial interest rates below 2% in 2005 and 2006 is from page 56 of the Winter 2009 issue of the *University of Colorado Law Review*, under the title "The Law & Economics of Subprime Lending." The rapid pace of home sales in California in 2004 and 2005 is from page 60 of the study *State of the California Housing Market 2008–2009*, published by the California Association of Realtors, while the fact that more than half of the homes sold during these two years received multiple offers from prospective buyers is from page 33. The high percentage of homes purchased as investments in 2005 and 2006 was mentioned on page 33 of the Winter 2009 issue of the *University of Colorado Law Review*, under the title "The Law & Economics of Subprime Lending." The description of the general characteristics of subprime borrowers is from pages 55–56 of the same article, while the statement that the great majority of adjustable rate subprime mortgages entered foreclosure before a rise in interest rates occurred is from page 28. The description of mortgage-backed securities as a "blizzard of increasingly complex new securities" is from page 11 of *Financial Shock* by Mark Zandi. The statement that the Federal Reserve does not have a specific definition for "predatory lending" is from page 345, note 2 of the Summer 2005 issue of the *Federal Reserve Bulletin*, under the title "New Information Reported under HMDA and Its Application in Fair Lending Enforcement."

CHAPTER 2: The Politics of the Housing Boom

Pressures on Fannie Mae from the Clinton Administration to expand lending to low and moderate income borrowers were mentioned on page C2 of the September 30, 1999 issue of the *New York Times*, under the headline "Fannie Mae Eases Credit to Aid Mortgage Lending." Data on the affordability of homes as measured by comparing home prices to income in Youngstown, Ohio, Las Vegas and San Diego are from pages 30, 33, and 34 of the study *4th Annual Demographia International Housing Affordability Survey: 2008*. Newspaper accounts depicting the lack of affordable housing as a nationwide problem are from page A18 of the July 5, 2002 issue of the *New York Times*, under the headline "Facing Up to the Housing Crisis," and also page B7 of the June 9, 2002 issue of the *Washington Post*, in a column titled "Housing on the Back Burner." J.A. Schumpeter's quote is from page 529 of his *History of Economic Analysis*. The news report highlighting the increased affordability of housing in most of the nation is from page A1 of the December 29, 2005 issue of the *New York Times*, under the headline "Twenty Years Later, Buying a House Is Less of a Bite." The findings of the Heritage Foundation study can be found on page 9 of the August 22, 1990 *Backgrounder*, No. 783, titled "Washington's Continuing Fiction: A National Housing Shortage." Information on the affordability of housing in the United States is from pages 24–30 of the Fall 2002 issue of *Regulation*, in an article titled "Zoning's Steep Price," and also pages 117–118 of *The Best-Laid Plans* by Randal O'Toole. Data showing that for the United States as a whole, home costs have not exceeded 25% of a home buyer's income since 1985 can be found on page 33 of the report *The State of the Nation's Housing 2008*, published by the Joint Center for Housing Studies of Harvard University in 2008. That the median home price in America is 3.6 times the median income of Americans, while the median home prices in Britain, Australia and New Zealand take a much higher share of these countries' median income, was shown on

page 11 of *4th Annual Demographia International Housing Affordability Survey: 2008.*
Data on housing's share of American consumer spending in 1901 and in 2002–2003
are from pages 6 and 63 of *100 Years of U.S. Consumer Spending: Data for the Nation,
New York City, and Boston*, Report 991 of the U.S. Department of Labor. The
statement that until 1970, median home prices in the United States were about
twice as much as the median family income is from page 117 of *The Best-Laid Plans*
by Randal O'Toole, while the affordability of housing in San Francisco in 1969 is
discussed on page 118. The increase in the ratio between home prices and income
in San Jose, California, from 1969 to 2005 is from page 8 of the October 17, 2007
issue of *Policy Analysis*, No. 602, in an article titled "Do You Know the Way to L.A.?:
San Jose Shows How to Turn an Urban Area into Los Angeles in Three Stressful
Decades." The fact that 23 of the 26 "severely unaffordable" international urban
areas follow "smart-growth" policies is from page 38 of the study "The Planning
Penalty: How Smart Growth Makes Housing Unaffordable," written by Randal
O'Toole and published by the Independent Institute in 2006. The purpose of the
Community Reinvestment Act of 1977 is quoted from Section 802 of Title VIII of
the Act of October 12, 1977 (Public Law 95–128; 91 Stat. 1147), *United States
Statutes at Large, 1977*, Volume 91, published by the United States Government
Printing Office in 1980. Attorney General Janet Reno's warnings to banks whose
lending patterns were believed to be racially biased based on statistical disparities
are from page B7 of the December 14, 1993 issue of the *Washington Times*, in an
article titled "Bank to Pay $960,000 in Loan-Bias Settlement," and page A2 of the
December 14, 1993 issue of the *Wall Street Journal*, under the headline "Shawmut
Settles Charges of Bias in Its Lending." The high rate of default and foreclosure
among minority homeowners during the housing bust is discussed on page 15 of the
study "Subprime Mortgages, Foreclosures, and Urban Neighborhoods," Working
Paper 2009–1, published by the Federal Reserve Bank of Atlanta in February 2009,
page A12 of the January 8, 2008 issue of the *New York Times*, under the headline
"Baltimore Is Suing Bank Over Foreclosure Crisis," page B3 of the May 4, 2008
issue of the *Orlando Sentinel*, in an article titled "Foreclosure Crisis Hits Hard in
Black Communities," pages A1 and A10 of the January 5, 2009 issue of the *Wall
Street Journal*, in a story titled "Housing Push for Hispanics Spawns Wave of
Foreclosures," and page A1 of the November 4, 2007 issue of the *Atlanta Journal-
Constitution*, under the headline "Black Atlantans Frequently Snared by Subprime

Loans." The new regulations that were enacted in 1995 to expand lending to low-and moderate-income borrowers are mentioned on page 23 of the February 2009 issue of *The American Spectator*, in an article titled "The True Origins of This Financial Crisis." The insistence of the Clinton Administration that banks with unsatisfactory ratings under the 1977 Community Reinvestment Act be prohibited from diversifying their business is from page A3 of the October 22, 1999 issue of the *Wall Street Journal*, under the headline "Glass-Steagall Overhaul Remains on Hold." That a satisfactory record of meeting community credit needs was required of banks seeking to diversify their business is quoted from the Gramm-Leach-Bliley Act of November 12, 1999 (Public Law 106–102; 113 Stat. 1350). The increased pressures imposed by the Department of Housing and Urban Development upon lenders during the 1990s are mentioned on page 6 of "How Did We Get into This Financial Mess?" *Cato Institute Briefing Papers*, No. 110, November 18, 2008. The concessions made by banks to community activist groups were discussed in the *Wall Street Journal*, September 10, 1987, section 2, page 35, under the headline "Public Service or Blackmail? Banks Pressed to Finance Local Projects." The pledge by Sumitomo Bank of California to give 20% to 25% of its contracts to minority-owned businesses was reported on page A22 of the January 6, 1999 issue of the *Wall Street Journal*, under the headline "Gramm's Glass-Steagall Beef." The quote from Fannie Mae CEO Franklin Raines is from page C2 of the September 30, 1999 issue of the *New York Times*, under the headline "Fannie Mae Eases Credit to Aid Mortgage Lending." President George W. Bush's efforts to increase home ownership were discussed on page 31 of the August 23, 2004 issue of *Barron's*, under the headline "Nothing Down." The decline in the proportion of 30-year fixed-rate mortgages from 2001 to 2006 and the increase in subprime loans are from page 4 of the November 2008 *Financial Services Outlook*, published by the American Enterprise Institute, and the extent of subprime and non-traditional loans purchased by Fannie Mae and Freddie Mac from 2005 to 2007 is noted on page 5. The Department of Housing and Urban Development's impact on Fannie Mae and Freddie Mac was described on pages A1 and A2 of the June 10, 2008 issue of the *Washington Post*, in an article titled "How HUD Mortgage Policy Fed the Crisis." The magnitude of the mortgage guarantees of Fannie Mae and Freddie Mac was reported on page 1 of the May 2005 *Financial Services Outlook*, published by the American Enterprise Institute. Information on the rankings of Gross Domestic

Product by nation is from page 26 of the *Pocket World in Figures*, 2008 Edition, published by *The Economist*. My discussion of the problems and risks during the housing boom was published on page A13 of the May 26, 2005 issue of the *Wall Street Journal*, under the headline "Cross Country: Froth in Frisco or Another Bubble?" Warnings of an impending decline in American home prices were issued on page 68 of the September 13, 2003 issue of *The Economist*, in an article titled "Hot Property." Concerns about the high costs of American homes and the risks to investors at large should those prices fall are from page 13 of the June 18, 2005 issue of *The Economist*, under the headline "After the Fall." The testimony of Treasury Secretary John W. Snow can be found on page 11 of *Hearing Before the Committee on Financial Services: U.S. House of Representatives*, One Hundred Eighth Congress, first session, September 10, 2003 and also page 33 of *Hearing Before the Committee on Financial Services: U.S. House of Representatives*, One Hundred Ninth Congress, first session, April 13, 2005. That 3,000 banks in the United States held government-sponsored enterprises debt equal to all their capital is from page 41 of the September 8, 2003 issue of *Newsweek*, in a column titled "Fixing Fannie and Freddie." The quote from Josh Rosner about the risks posed by pushing homeownership on people that were financially unqualified is from section 3, pages 1 and 9 of the October 3, 2004 issue of the *New York Times*, in an article titled "A Coming Nightmare of Homeownership?" The statement that the housing market was "losing touch with reality" and concerns that a downturn in housing prices posed significant risks to the economy are from pages 92 and 93 of the September 20, 2004 issue of *Fortune*, in an article titled "Is the Housing Boom Over?" Concerns over massive defaults and costs to taxpayers if Fannie Mae and Freddie Mac were not reined in are from page 8 of the May 2005 *Financial Services Outlook*, published by the American Enterprise Institute. The criticisms of President George W. Bush's efforts to increase home ownership can be found on page 31 of the August 23, 2004 issue of *Barron's*, under the title "Nothing Down." The concerns expressed by the Chair of the Federal Deposit Insurance Corporation (FDIC) about problem loans and higher-risk loans are from page 13 of *Hearing Before the Committee on Banking, Housing, and Urban Affairs: United States Senate*, One Hundred Seventh Congress, first session, June 20, 2001. Federal Reserve Chairman Alan Greenspan's testimony about the housing market is quoted from pages 5 and 6 of *Hearing Before the Joint Economic Committee: Congress of the United States*, One

Hundred Ninth Congress, first session, June 9, 2005. Greenspan's concerns about the risks posed by the growth of Fannie Mae and Freddie Mac were reported on pages 19 and 31 of *Hearing Before the Committee on Financial Services: U.S. House of Representatives*, One Hundred Ninth Congress, first session, February 17, 2005. His comment about turmoil in the financial markets is from page 1 of the September 17, 2007 issue of the *Financial Times* (London), in an article titled "Greenspan Alert on Homes," and his statements about the prevalence of subprime loans are from page B1 of the September 14, 2007 issue of *USA Today*, under the headline "Greenspan Slow to See Subprime Danger." Congressman Barney Frank's comments about the role played by Fannie Mae and Freddie Mac in creating affordable housing are from page 3 of *Hearing Before the Committee on Financial Services: U.S. House of Representatives*, One Hundred Eighth Congress, first session, September 10, 2003. His comments about subsidized housing are from pages 97 and 98 of *Hearing Before the Committee on Financial Services: U.S. House of Representatives*, One Hundred Eighth Congress, first session, September 25, 2003. Congressman Barney Frank's fears that concerns about the soundness of Fannie Mae and Freddie Mac might reduce affordable housing can be found on page 3 of *Hearing Before the Committee on Financial Services: U.S. House of Representatives*, One Hundred Eighth Congress, first session, September 10, 2003. His statements that there was no government bailout guaranteed if Fannie Mae and Freddie Mac failed are from the same page. Details on the costs of the bailout of Fannie Mae and Freddie Mac can be found on page A14 of the January 29, 2009 issue of the *Wall Street Journal*, under the headline "Fan and Fred's Lunch Tab," and also page 11 of *The Budget and Economic Outlook: Fiscal Years 2009 to 2019*, released by the Congressional Budget Office on January 8, 2009. Senator Christopher Dodd's comments on Fannie Mae and Freddie Mac are from page 454 of *Hearings Before the Committee on Banking, Housing, and Urban Affairs: United States Senate*, One Hundred Eighth Congress, first and second sessions, February 25, 2004. Senator Dodd's characterization of President Bush's calls for Fannie Mae and Freddie Mac to undergo reform as "ill-advised" is from pages C1 and C4 of the August 11, 2007 issue of the *New York Times*, under the headline "Fannie Mae's Offer to Help Ease Credit Squeeze Is Rejected, as Critics Complain of Opportunism." Senator Dodd's remarks from July 2008, that Fannie Mae and Freddie Mac were on "a sound footing" are from page S6594 of the July 11, 2008 *Congressional Record: Senate*.

Details of the government takeover of Fannie Mae and Freddie Mac are from pages A1 and A15 of the September 8, 2008 issue of the *Wall Street Journal,* under the headline "U.S. Seizes Mortgage Giants." The remarks of Congresswoman Maxine Waters are from page 9 of *Hearing Before the Committee on Financial Services: U.S. House of Representatives,* One Hundred Eighth Congress, first session, September 25, 2003. Congressman Joe Baca's statement that debates on the regulation of Fannie Mae and Freddie Mac could restrict access to minority homeownership are from page 86 of *Hearing Before the Committee on Financial Services: U.S. House of Representatives,* One Hundred Eighth Congress, first session, September 10, 2003. The letter from 76 House Democrats dated June 28, 2004, to President Bush urging his Administration to abandon its criticisms of the government-sponsored enterprises can be accessed from the web site of the House Committee on Financial Services at http://financialservices.house.gov/LtrBushGSEs.pdf. Testimony from the representative of the National Association of Homebuilders is from pages 83 and 84 of *Hearing Before the Committee on Financial Services: U.S. House of Representatives,* One Hundred Eighth Congress, first session, September 25, 2003. Testimony from an official of the National Urban League calling for increased affordable housing for minorities is from pages 90–91 of the same hearing. The testimony from the Director of Freddie Mac is from pages 42 and 44, while the comments of Fannie Mae's CEO Franklin Raines are from pages 45 and 46 of the same hearing. Details of the accounting irregularities uncovered at Fannie Mae in 2004 by the Office of Federal Housing Enterprise Oversight (OFHEO) and the subsequent investigation of OFHEO at the request of Republican Senator Kit Bond are from pages 13–14 of the September 27, 2004 issue of *Barron's,* under the title "Fannie Whacked," pages E1 and E2 of the November 20, 2004 issue of the *Washington Post,* under the headline "Freddie Mac Problems Led to Tougher OFHEO," and page C2 of the November 23, 2004 issue of the *New York Times,* in an article titled "Congress Urges Ouster of 2 Regulators." Congressman Frank's statement calling for a change of leadership at OFHEO was quoted on page E2 of the November 20, 2004 issue of the *Washington Post,* in the previously mentioned article "Freddie Mac Problems Led to Tougher OFHEO." The donations made to members of Congress by the employees and political action committees of Fannie Mae and Freddie Mac were reported on page A10 of a story beginning on the front page of the October 5, 2008 issue of the *St. Louis Post-Dispatch,* under the headline

"Bond's Tough Talk on Fannie, Freddie Rings Hollow to Some." The statement by Rep. Chris Shays on the power and influence wielded by Fannie Mae was quoted on page A2 of the November 22, 2004 issue of the *Wall Street Journal*, in an article titled "Fannie, Freddie Regulator Is Split Over Moves to Toughen Oversight." The political protection enjoyed by Fannie Mae and Freddie Mac, including the limitations imposed on their regulator, the Office of Federal Housing Enterprise Oversight (OFHEO), and the less strict capital requirements placed on these government-sponsored enterprises were discussed on pages A1 and A12 of the September 14, 2008 issue of the *Washington Post*, under the headline "How Washington Failed to Rein In Fannie, Freddie." The favorable terms on loans that Senator Christopher Dodd received from Countrywide Financial Corporation were mentioned on page A11 of the June 13, 2008 issue of the *Wall Street Journal*, under the title "Dodd Tied to Countrywide Loans," and page A14 of the February 3, 2009 issue of the *Wall Street Journal*, under the title "Dodd's Peek-A-Boo Disclosure." Senator Bob Bennett's ties to Fannie Mae and Freddie Mac were reported in the Politics section of the September 12, 2008 issue of the *Salt Lake Tribune*, under the headline "Background on Big Mortgage Takeover Targets." The statement that Fannie Mae and Freddie Mac hired ex-politicians is from page 80 of the July 19, 2008 issue of *The Economist*, in an article titled "A Brief Family History: Toxic Fudge." The granting of $12 million of TARP funds to Boston's OneUnited Bank after Congressman Barney Frank's intervention was reported on page A1 of the January 22, 2009 issue of the *Wall Street Journal*, under the headline "Political Interference Seen in Bank Bailout Decisions." Congresswoman Maxine Waters' ties to OneUnited Bank were reported on the front page of the March 13, 2009 issue of the *New York Times*, under the headline "A Representative, Her Ties and a Bank Meeting." Gerald P. O'Driscoll's comments on Fannie Mae and Freddie Mac are from the September 9, 2008 issue of the *New York Post*, under the headline "Fannie/Freddie Bailout Baloney."

CHAPTER 3: The Housing Bust

Robert J. Samuelson's quote is from page 37 of the February 25, 2002 issue of *Newsweek*, under the headline "The Last Great Bull Market." Details on the

Federal Reserve System and the rise in interest rates between 2004–2006 are from pages A1 and C8 of the June 30, 2006 issue of the *New York Times*, in an article titled "Fed Raises Rates, But Scales Back Talk of Inflation." The rise in mortgage interest rates following the increase of the Federal Reserve's interest rates was noted on page 35 of the Winter 2009 issue of the *University of Colorado Law Review*, in an article titled "The Law & Economics of Subprime Lending." That home prices declined for the first time in more than a decade in 2006 was reported on page D1 of the October 26, 2006 issue of the *Wall Street Journal*, under the headline "Home Prices Keep Sliding; Buyers Sit Tight." The high rates of foreclosure among counties in California in 2006 were reported on page C1 of the October 14, 2006 issue of the *San Francisco Chronicle*, under the headline "Foreclosure Activity Skyrockets in East Bay." The 87 percent increase in foreclosures filed nationally in June 2007, as well as the near tripling of foreclosures in the Bay Area were reported on pages C1 and C2 of the July 12, 2007 issue of the *San Francisco Chronicle*, in an article titled "Foreclosure Activity Rises Dramatically." The 800 percent increase in the number of California homes reverting to bank ownership in 2007 was reported on pages C1 and C2 of the July 25, 2007 issue of the *San Francisco Chronicle*, under the headline "Foreclosures Go Through the Roof." The $40,000 cost to banks to foreclose on a loan was reported on pages C1 and C6 of the March 31, 2007 issue of the *New York Times*, in an article titled "Lenders May Prove Adjustable." That half of all existing homes sold in the San Francisco Bay Area in December 2008 were homes that had been foreclosed was reported on the front page of the January 22, 2009 issue of the *San Francisco Chronicle*, under the headline "Foreclosures Fuel Home Sales Surge," while the near 47% decline in home prices in the Bay Area was reported on page A12 of the same article. The contrast between the boom and bust years in Phoenix, Arizona, was reported in a front-page story in the November 7, 2006 issue of the *New York Times*, under the headline "After Arizona's Housing Boom, 'For Sale' Is a Sign of the Times." The record-setting decline in the Standard & Poor's home-price index was reported on page A2 of the December 31, 2008 issue of the *Wall Street Journal*, under the headline "Home Prices Declined at Record Pace in October." The steep declines in home prices in coastal California, as well as in Las Vegas, Miami, and Phoenix during 2008 were reported in a December 30, 2008 press release issued by Standard & Poor's titled "Home Price Declines Worsen as We Enter the Fourth Quarter of 2008 According to the S&P/Case-Shiller

Home Price Indices." That California was home to 16 of the 25 metropolitan areas with the steepest home-price declines was reported on page A13 of a story beginning on the front page of the October 22, 2008 issue of the *Wall Street Journal*, under the headline "California Home Sales Revive, But Not Without Intense Pain." The $100,000 price decline in California homes from 2007 to 2008 was reported on page 63 of *State of the California Housing Market 2008–2009*, published by the California Association of Realtors. The dramatic home price increases in San Diego from 2000 to 2005 were reported on page 40 of the October 16, 2006 issue of *Newsweek*, under the headline "The Worrying Housing Bust," while the home price declines from 2006 to 2008 were reported on page C1 of the December 31, 2008 issue of the *San Diego Union-Tribune*, under the headline "Home Prices Down 26.7% from Year Ago." The extent of home price declines in the United States as measured by various indices was shown on pages 8–9 of *The State of the Nation's Housing: 2008*, published by the Joint Center for Housing Studies of Harvard University in 2008. That there were great disparities in the severity of home price declines among different metropolitan areas was shown on page 8 of the same report. The low rate of decline of home prices in Dallas during the housing bust, and its affordability during the boom years, were reported on page A2 of the December 31, 2008 issue of the *Wall Street Journal*, under the headline "Home Prices Declined at Record Pace in October," and pages A1 and C9 of the December 29, 2005 issue of the *New York Times*, in an article titled "Twenty Years Later, Buying a House Is Less of a Bite." The quote from Alan Greenspan about "local bubbles" in housing markets in the United States is from a front-page story in the May 23, 2005 issue of the *Wall Street Journal*, under the headline "As Prices Rise, Homeowners Go Deep in Debt to Buy Real Estate." That 55% of borrowers who financed a home purchase with an option ARM owed more than the value of their home, and that 28 percent of such mortgages were delinquent or in foreclosure was reported on page C1 of the January 30, 2009 issue of the *Wall Street Journal*, in an article titled "Option ARMs See Rising Defaults." The decline in the proportion of 30-year fixed-rate mortgages to just one-third of all mortgages was reported on page 4 of the November 2008 *Financial Services Outlook*, published by the American Enterprise Institute. The high rate of delinquency among borrowers with adjustable-rate loans, interest-only loans, and payment-option loans was shown on page 19 of *The State of the Nation's Housing 2008*, published by the Joint Center for

Housing Studies of Harvard University in 2008. Federal Reserve Board Chairman Ben Bernanke's testimony is from page 12 of *Hearing Before the Committee on Financial Services: U.S. House of Representatives*, One Hundred Tenth Congress, first session, September 20, 2007. The statement that minority homeowners took out a disproportionate share of subprime loans is from page C4 of the December 20, 2006 issue of the *New York Times*, under the headline "Study Predicts Foreclosure for 1 in 5 Subprime Loans." The high rate of foreclosures among minority homeowners during the housing bust was reported on page 15 of "Subprime Mortgages, Foreclosures, and Urban Neighborhoods," Working Paper 2009–1, published by the Federal Reserve Bank of Atlanta in February 2009; page A12 of the January 8, 2008 issue of the *New York Times*, under the headline "Baltimore Is Suing Bank Over Foreclosure Crisis"; page B3 of the May 4, 2008 issue of the *Orlando Sentinel*, in an article titled "Foreclosure Crisis Hits Hard in Black Communities"; pages A1 and A10 of the January 5, 2009 issue of the *Wall Street Journal*, in a story titled "Housing Push for Hispanics Spawns Wave of Foreclosures"; page A1 of the November 4, 2007 issue of the *Atlanta Journal-Constitution*, under the title "Black Atlantans Frequently Snared by Subprime Loans"; and page B1 of the April 26, 2007 issue of *USA Today*, under the headline "In 2005, Half of Minorities Purchased Their Homes with Subprime Loans." The high number of foreclosed properties owned by speculators in the San Francisco Bay Area, Las Vegas, Arizona, and Florida was reported on pages A1 and A10 of the December 16, 2007 issue of the *San Francisco Chronicle*, in an article titled "Foreclosures: How Megaflipping Flopped." The remarks of Holman Jenkins are from page A15 of the February 18, 2009 issue of the *Wall Street Journal*, under the headline "How Democracy Ruined the Bailout." The German bank that had to be bailed out by regulators due to losses on U.S. subprime mortgages was mentioned on page A18 of the October 31, 2007 issue of the *Wall Street Journal* in a news story that began on the front page under the headline "Bernanke, In First Crisis, Rewrites Fed Playbook." The impact of the subprime crisis on Wall Street was discussed on page 52 of the Winter 2009 issue of the *University of Colorado Law Review*, in an article titled "The Law & Economics of Subprime Lending." Some investors' lack of knowledge about the risks of subprime mortgages was mentioned on page 27 of "The Subprime Panic," Working Paper 14398, published by the National Bureau of Economic Research in October 2008. The statement that the purchase of mortgage-backed securities was "a leap in the dark" is from page 13 of a special report (with its own separate page numbers) titled "Greed–and Fear" within the January 24, 2009 issue of *The Economist*. The more than five-fold increase in the value of subprime mortgages from 1995 to 2003 was shown on page 20 of the Winter 2009 issue of the *University of Colorado Law Review*, under the title "The Law & Economics of Subprime Lending." The process of gaining the highest rating for mortgage-backed securities by "shopping" them to the three major rating agencies was mentioned on page 54 of the same study. The fact that loans made under the Community Reinvestment Act were just 7% of the loans made by Bank of America but represented 29% of its losses on mortgages is from page 36 of the same article. The quote from Professor Stanley Liebowitz is from page 24 of the February 2009 issue of *The American Spectator*, under the headline "The True Origins of This Financial Crisis." That there were 30 state examiners to watch over thousands of consumer finance companies in California, and that as a result mortgage companies were inspected only about once every four years, is from pages 154–155 of *Financial Shock* by Mark Zandi. The political pressures imposed on these regulators were mentioned on page 155 of the same book. The increase in the ratio of homes sold in California costing less than half a million dollars from 2007 to 2008 was reported on page 4 of *State of the California Housing Market 2008–2009*, published by the California Association of Realtors. The amount of a down payment as a percentage of the sales price of California homes in 2006 compared with 2008 was reported on page 14 of the same report. The decline of zero down payment mortgages in California from 2007 to 2008 was reported on page 15 of the same report. The declining share of interest-only adjustable rate mortgages in California from 2007 to 2008 was shown on page 16 of the same report. That fixed-rate mortgages rose from 55 percent of all mortgages in California in 2005 to more than 90 percent of the state's mortgages in 2008 was shown on page 61 of the same report. The dramatic decrease in the share of first-time California home buyers resorting to second mortgages to finance a home purchase from 2006 to 2008 was shown on page 18 of that same report. The steep drop in the share of adjustable rate mortgages nationally from 2004 to 2007 is from page 161 of the *Financial Services Fact Book, 2009*, published by the Insurance Information Institute. The dramatic decline in the value of subprime mortgages from 2006 to 2007 is shown on page 19 of the report *The State of the Nation's Housing 2008*, published by the Joint Center for Housing Studies of Harvard University in

2008. The increased selectivity of lenders and mortgage insurers in the wake of the housing bust is discussed on pages B1 and B5 of the January 24, 2009 issue of the *New York Times*, under the title "Costs and Tighter Rules Thwart Refinancings." Accusations by members of the Senate Banking Committee of greed on Wall Street, and their criticisms of lax regulatory oversight were reported on page A24 of the September 24, 2008 issue of the *New York Times*, under the headline "In a Crisis, Senatorial Rhetoric Bursts Forth." The hearing before the House Financial Services Committee in which leaders of the country's largest banks were "hectored" by lawmakers was reported on page C1 of the February 12, 2009 issue of the *Los Angeles Times*, in an article titled "Economic Crisis: Lawmakers Give Banks a Scolding." Senator Christopher Dodd's criticism of the Bush Administration is quoted from page A15 of the September 12, 2008 issue of the *Washington Post*, under the headline "Where Was Sen. Dodd?" Senator Dodd's remarks about Alan Greenspan can be found on page 124 of the September 17, 2007 issue of *Fortune*, in an article titled "Oh, the People You'll Blame!" Senator Christopher Dodd's favorable comments about Fannie Mae and Freddie Mac are from his opening statement from the February 7, 2008 hearing "Reforming the Regulation of the Government Sponsored Enterprises." (Senator Dodd's remarks as prepared were released in a press release by the U.S. Senate Banking Committee.) Republican Senator Robert Bennett of Utah likewise depicted Fannie Mae and Freddie Mac as enterprises that "emerge as the heroes because they're the only ones with money left." Senator Bennett's remarks are from page 3 of the Washington section of the March 7, 2008 issue of the *American Banker*, under the title "GSE Reform Hearing Turns to Broader Debate Over Bailout." Details on the costs of the bailout of Fannie Mae and Freddie Mac can be found on page A14 of the January 29, 2009 issue of the *Wall Street Journal*, under the title "Fan and Fred's Lunch Tab." Data on the costs of the bailouts of Bank of America, Citigroup, J.P. Morgan Chase, and Wells Fargo are from pages 78–79 of the February 16, 2009 issue of *Fortune*, in an article titled "The World According to TARP." Senator Christopher Dodd's statements that Fannie Mae and Freddie Mac were "fundamentally strong" are quoted from page A10 of the July 12–13, 2008 issue of the *Wall Street Journal*, under the headline "Fannie Mae Ugly." The editorial critical of Senator Christopher Dodd appears on page A12 of the July 21, 2008 issue of the *Wall Street Journal*, under the title "Fannie and Freddie's Enablers." Congressman Barney Frank's claim that the subprime crisis resulted from too little regulation is from page 11 of the August 20, 2007 issue of the *Financial Times* of London, under the title "A (Sub)Prime Argument for More Regulation." Congressman Frank's statements that bad decisions in the private sector and a conservative philosophy are what led to the financial crisis are from page D9 of the September 28, 2008 issue of the *Boston Globe*, under the title "Frank's Fingerprints Are All Over the Financial Fiasco." Congressman Frank's further statements that excessive deregulation caused the financial crisis can be found on page A17 of the July 11, 2008 issue of the *Washington Post*, under the title "Capitalism's Reality Check," and page A11 of the September 14, 2007 issue of the *Boston Globe*, under the title "Lessons of the Subprime Crisis." Senator Charles Schumer's statement that deregulation led to the financial crisis is from page S8991 of the September 18, 2008 *Congressional Record: Senate*. The exchange between Maria Bartiromo and Congressman Barney Frank is from page 20 of the December 22, 2008 issue of *BusinessWeek*, under the title "Facetime: Barney Frank on Detroit, Housing, and Executive Pay." Senator Kit Bond's comments are from page S8970 of the September 18, 2008 *Congressional Record: Senate*. The newspaper account detailing Senator Kit Bond's past efforts to obstruct the OFHEO can be found on the front page of the October 5, 2008 issue of the *St. Louis Post-Dispatch*, under the headline "Bond's Tough Talk on Fannie, Freddie Rings Hollow to Some." Senator Barbara Boxer's statement about judges modifying the loans on principal residences is from page S2259 of the April 1, 2008 *Congressional Record: Senate*. The legislation introduced by Congressman John Conyers and Senator Richard Durbin which would allow bankruptcy judges to modify home mortgages is mentioned on page A13 of the February 13, 2009 issue of the *Wall Street Journal*, under the title "Don't Let Judges Tear Up Mortgage Contracts." Senator Harry Reid's remarks about amending the Bankruptcy Code to allow judges to modify mortgage terms are from page S1218 of the February 27, 2008 *Congressional Record: Senate*. Republican Senator Mitch McConnell's proposal of granting government-backed, 4% fixed mortgages to credit-worthy borrowers, and Professor Edward Glaeser's criticisms of that proposal are from page A13 of the February 5, 2009 issue of the *Wall Street Journal*, under the title "The GOP Has a Dumb Mortgage Idea." Senator Christopher Dodd's discussions of foreclosure mitigation can be found on pages S1812, S1815–S1816, and S1831 of the February 6, 2009 *Congressional Record: Senate*. Senator Christopher Dodd's proposed legislation to improve the regulation of Fannie Mae and Freddie Mac and encourage more funding for affordable housing is from page A2 of the May 13, 2008 issue of the *Washington Post*, in an article titled "Senate Talks Collapse on a Housing Bill." Congressman Barney Frank's housing-rescue proposal is discussed on page 8 of the May 2008 issue of *Mortgage Banking*, in an article titled "Congress, Administration Each Propose FHA Mortgage Relief." That 43% of modified loans were again delinquent within eight months was reported on page 32 of the February 21, 2009 issue of *The Economist*, under the title "Can't Pay or Won't Pay?" Information on the $700 billion economic bailout package (TARP) signed by President Bush in 2008 can be found on pages A1 and A12 of the October 4, 2008 issue of the *New York Times*, under the headline "Bush Signs Bill," while information on the $787 billion stimulus package signed by President Obama in 2009 is from page A11 of the February 14, 2009 issue of the *New York Times*, in an article titled "A Smaller, Faster Stimulus Plan, but Still with a Lot of Money." Data on the costs of the bailouts of J.P. Morgan Chase, Wells Fargo, AIG, Bank of America, and Citigroup are from pages 78–79 of the February 16, 2009 issue of *Fortune*, in an article titled "The World According to TARP." Adam Smith's remarks on the misapplication of money set aside by government for a particular purpose can be found on page 873 of his *The Wealth of Nations*, Modern Library edition. David Ricardo's remarks on the same subject are from page 248 of Volume I and pages 194–195 of Volume IV of *The Works and Correspondence of David Ricardo*, edited by Piero Sraffa and published by Cambridge University Press. Data on the share of the American national debt that is foreign owned are from pages 240–241 of *Analytical Perspectives, Budget of the United States Government, Fiscal Year 2009*, published in 2008 by the U.S. Government Printing Office. The drop in business spending on equipment and software in the last quarter of 2008 was reported on page A10 of the January 31, 2009 issue of the *Wall Street Journal*, under the title "A Capital Strike." That banks were reluctant to lend money to borrowers after the Bush administration's bailout was noted on page B5 of the January 27, 2009 issue of the *New York Times*, from an article beginning on page B1 titled "Something to Fear, After All." The historic fall in monetary velocity is reported on page A10 of the January 31, 2009 issue of the *Wall Street Journal*, under the title "A Capital Strike." That January 2009 ranked as Wall Street's worst January ever was discussed on pages C1 and C3 of the January 31, 2009 issue of the *San Francisco*

Chronicle, under the title "Stocks Fall– Economy, Bank Fears," and page B1 of the January 31, 2009 issue of the *Wall Street Journal*, under the headline "January Was Dow's Worst In 113 Years." The continued decline in the stock market in February 2009 was reported on page A1 of the February 24, 2009 issue of the *Wall Street Journal*, under the headline "Stocks Drop to 50% of Peak." Discussion of the lack of clarity of the TARP legislation was from pages 28–29 of *Getting Off Track*, by John B. Taylor. President Obama's remarks leading up to Treasury Secretary Geithner's presentation of the Administration's bank stabilization plan are from the President's February 9, 2009 press conference. The lack of details in Treasury Secretary Geithner's plan was noted on page B8 of the February 11, 2009 issue of the *St. Louis Post-Dispatch*, under the headline "Son of TARP." The critical remarks from the *New York Times* are from page A26 of the February 11, 2009 issue, under the title "The Bailout's Next Chapter." Other critical assessments of Treasury Secretary Geithner's presentation can be found on page A17 of the February 13, 2009 issue of the *Washington Post*, under the title "Treasury's Salesman-in-Training," and also page D1 of the February 11, 2009 issue of the *Washington Post*, in an article titled "Geithner Plan Lacks Freshness and Clarity." The estimate by the Congressional Budget Office that it would be September 2010 before 74% of the stimulus funds were spent was reported on page A11 of the February 14, 2009 issue of the *New York Times*, under the headline "A Smaller, Faster Stimulus Plan, but Still with a Lot of Money." The comments from *The Economist* magazine about the stimulus plan are from page 13 of the February 14, 2009 issue, under the title "The Obama Rescue."

CHAPTER 4: Housing Mystiques and Housing Mistakes

The need for more affordable housing in the United States was stated on page 12 of the July 2002 issue of the *National Real Estate Investor*, in an article titled "Need for Affordable Housing Is Rising." The benefits of decent and affordable housing were described on page 1 of *Meeting Our Nation's Housing Challenges*, a report by the Bipartisan Millennial Housing Commission published in 2002. Jacob Riis' descriptions of the tenements of New York's lower east side as "nurseries of crime" are from pages 3 and 5 of his *How the Other Half Lives*, Harvard University Press edition. The fact that many of those living in tenements that were to be closed down had to be forcibly removed by the police was noted on page 14. Jacob Riis' observation that some people "carry their slums with them wherever they go" is from page 21 of the same book. That many middle-class blacks are opposed to housing voucher programs was noted on pages 84–91 of the Autumn 2000 issue of *City Journal*, under the title "Let's End Housing Vouchers." The Boston neighborhood described as "the worst slum in the city," but which also had low rates of delinquency, disease, and infant mortality was discussed on page 10 of *The Death and Life of Great American Cities* by Jane Jacobs. President George W. Bush's statements about encouraging home ownership are from a front-page story in the December 21, 2008 issue of the *New York Times*, under the headline "White House Philosophy Stoked Mortgage Bonfire." Criticisms of studies that claimed discrimination in lending can be found in Chapter 15 of *Backfire: A Reporter's Look at Affirmative Action*, written by Bob Zelnick, and pages 178–183 of my *Economic Facts and Fallacies*. See also a study titled "The Role of Race in Mortgage Lending: Revisiting the Boston Fed Study," a Working Paper published in December 1996 by the Division of Research and Statistics, Federal Reserve Board of Governors; "A Study That Deserves No Credit," on page A14 of the September 1, 1993 issue of the *Wall Street Journal*; and page 13 of the Mortgage section of the August 19, 1993 issue of *The American Banker*, under the title "Boston Fed's Bias Study Was Deeply Flawed." Information on the millions of dollars that Jesse Jackson's organizations have received from financial institutions over the years can be found on pages A1 and A11 of the March 27, 2001 issue of the *Washington Post*, in an article titled "Jackson's Fundraising Methods Spur Questions," page A16 of the July 29, 2008 issue of the *Wall Street Journal*, under the title "Fannie Mae's Political Immunity," and pages 20–21 of the May 27, 2002 issue of *Insight*, in an article titled "Freddie Mac, Verizon Made Jesse's Hit List." Efforts by the group ACORN to compel banks to extend more loans to low- and moderate income families under the Community Reinvestment Act are mentioned on page A22 of the October 25, 2008 issue of the *Los Angeles Times*, under the title "Don't Blame the Victims." Congressman Paul Broun's criticism of ACORN is from page H1018 of the February 4, 2009 *Congressional Record: House*. Congressman Barney Frank's defense of community activists who challenge banks on their lending standards is from page

H11541 of the November 4, 1999 *Congressional Record: House*. Approval rates for black and white borrowers seeking government-backed, conventional, and refinancing loans can be found on pages 870 and 871 of the November 1991 issue of the *Federal Reserve Bulletin*, in an article titled "Home Mortgage Disclosure Act: Expanded Data on Residential Lending." The limitations of the data in the Federal Reserve System's mortgage study are described on page 859 of the same article. Newspaper editorials claiming discrimination in lending based on the findings of the Federal Reserve's study can be found on page A12 of the October 23, 1991 issue of *USA Today*, under the title "Discrimination and Loans," and also page C2 of the October 25, 1991 issue of the *St. Louis Post-Dispatch*, under the title "Racial Gap Persists in Mortgage Lending." News accounts claiming discrimination in mortgage lending include a front-page story from the March 31, 1992 issue of the *Wall Street Journal*, under the headline "Behind the Figures: Federal Data Detail Pervasive Racial Gap In Mortgage Lending," and also a story from page D1 of the October 22, 1991 issue of the *New York Times*, under the title "Racial Gap Detailed on Mortgages." That income was the only financial characteristic of loan applicants in the Federal Reserve's study was noted on page 867 of the November 1991 issue of the *Federal Reserve Bulletin*, in an article titled "Home Mortgage Disclosure Act: Expanded Data on Residential Lending," while the factors that lenders must evaluate in considering a loan applicant's ability to repay a loan are discussed on page 875. Data on disparities in net worth between blacks and whites in the highest income quintile are shown on page 14 of "Net Worth and the Assets of Households: 2002," *Current Population Reports*, P70–115, published by the U.S. Census Bureau in April 2008. The differences between blacks and whites in inherited wealth are reported on page 1334 of the March 2002 issue of the *American Journal of Sociology*, under the title "Lifetime Inheritances of Three Generations of Whites and Blacks." That whites were denied conventional mortgage loans more often than Asian Americans was shown on page 870 of the November 1991 issue of the *Federal Reserve Bulletin*, under the title "Home Mortgage Disclosure Act: Expanded Data on Residential Lending," and also on page 808 of the November 1992 issue of the *Federal Reserve Bulletin*, under the title "Expanded HMDA Data on Residential Lending: One Year Later." Data showing that white borrowers resorted to subprime loans more often than Asian American borrowers are from page 379 of the Summer 2005 issue of the *Federal Reserve Bulletin*, under the title "New Information

Reported under HMDA and Its Application in Fair Lending Enforcement," and also page 5 of the November 2007 - Brief #2 published by the Joint Center for Political and Economic Studies under the title "African Americans and Homeownership: The Subprime Lending Experience, 1995 to 2007." The higher credit scores of Asian Americans compared to whites were reported on page 80 of a report by the Board of Governors of the Federal Reserve System titled *Report to the Congress on Credit Scoring and Its Effects on the Availability and Affordability of Credit*, submitted to the Congress pursuant to section 215 of the Fair and Accurate Credit Transactions Act of 2003, published in August 2007. The frequency with which blacks, whites, Hispanics, and Asians resorted to subprime loans in the metro Atlanta area was reported on page A12 of the November 6, 2007 issue of the *Atlanta Journal-Constitution*, under the title "Answers to Credit Woes Are Not In Black and White." The news story comparing the frequency with which black and white borrowers used subprime loans is from page A2 of the April 11, 2005 issue of the *Washington Post*, in an article titled "Disparities Found in Sub-Prime Lending." The conclusions of the 2002 study that included credit history among its variables in studying mortgage default can be found on page 18 of "New Evidence on the Relationship Between Race and Mortgage Default: The Importance of Credit History Data," prepared by Unicon Research Corporation and published on May 23, 2002. That many factors considered in credit underwriting and pricing are absent from HMDA data was noted on page A158 of the September 2006 issue of the *Federal Reserve Bulletin*, in an article titled "Higher-Priced Home Lending and the 2005 HMDA Data." The greater incidence of higher priced loans among black and Hispanic borrowers as compared to whites, and data showing that Asian Americans were the group who resorted to such loans least of all appeared on page A159 of the same article. The findings of the study of mortgage lending in Boston can be found on page 2 of "Mortgage Lending in Boston: Interpreting HMDA Data," Working Paper No. 92–7, October 1992, published by the Federal Reserve Bank of Boston. News stories claiming discrimination in lending following the release of the Boston Fed's study can be found on page 1 of the Economy section of the October 9, 1992 issue of the *Boston Globe*, in an article titled "Study Shows Racial Bias in Lending," and also page A3 of the October 9, 1992 issue of the *Wall Street Journal*, under the title "Boston Fed Finds Racial Discrimination in Mortgage Lending Is Still Widespread." The remarks by the head of the Federal Reserve

Bank of Boston can be found on page 48 of the January 4, 1993 issue of *Forbes*, in an article titled "The Hidden Clue." The conclusion by the Federal Reserve in Washington that the claims of discrimination in the 1992 Boston Fed study were "difficult to justify" was stated on page 1 of the study "The Role of Race in Mortgage Lending: Revisiting the Boston Fed Study," a Working Paper published in December 1996 by the Division of Research and Statistics, Federal Reserve Board of Governors. The fact that blacks and Hispanics in Boston were more likely to buy lower-priced homes than whites at a time when banks were concerned about home prices declining especially sharply in such houses was reported on page 13 of the Mortgage section of the August 19, 1993 issue of *The American Banker*, under the title "Boston Fed's Bias Study Was Deeply Flawed." Nobel-Prizewinning economist Gary Becker's assessment of the Boston Federal Reserve study can be found on page 18 of the April 19, 1993 issue of *BusinessWeek*, under the title "The Evidence Against Banks Doesn't Prove Bias." Information on the sex discrimination case brought by the EEOC against Sears can be found on page 77 of the May 25, 1992 issue of *Forbes*, under the title "Spiral of Silence," and also *E.E.O.C. v. Sears, Roebuck & Co.*, 839 F.2d 302 at 360. The Justice Department's discrimination case against Decatur Federal Savings & Loan was discussed on page C18 of the September 18, 1992 issue of the *Wall Street Journal*, in an article titled "Decatur Federal Settles U.S. Charge of Racial Bias in Mortgage Lending." The Federal Reserve Board's refusal to grant permission to Shawmut National Corporation to acquire New Dartmouth Bank was reported in section 3, page 4 of the November 28, 1993 issue of the *New York Times*, in an article titled "Lending-Bias Rules Create Quandary for Banks." The $960,000 settlement paid by the mortgage subsidiary of Shawmut National Corporation, and the warnings issued by Attorney General Janet Reno to lenders are from page B7 of the December 14, 1993 issue of the *Washington Times*, in an article titled "Bank to Pay $960,000 in Loan-Bias Settlement." That the Federal Reserve withdrew its opposition to Shawmut's acquisition of the New Dartmouth Bank following Shawmut's near million dollar settlement with the Justice Department was reported on page A24 of the December 20, 1993 issue of the *Washington Times*, under the headline "How to Rob a Bank Legally," while the fact that no individual complaints were filed by minorities claiming they had been discriminated against was also noted in the same column. The Justice Department's settlement with Chevy Chase Federal Savings

Bank requiring the bank to open new branches in minority neighborhoods was discussed on page D1 of the August 23, 1994 issue of the *New York Times*, under the title "Wider Attack on Loan Bias Seen in Accord with S.& L." The decline of the black population in San Francisco since 1970 was discussed on the front page of the April 9, 2007 issue of the *San Francisco Chronicle*, under the headline "S.F. Moves to Stem African American Exodus." Data on declining black population by at least 10,000 in each of four counties between the 1990 and the 2000 censuses are shown in the following Census publications: *1990 Census of Population: General Population Characteristics California*, 1990 CP–1–6, Section 1 of 3, pages 27, 28, 30, and 31; *Profiles of General Demographic Characteristics 2000* (2000 Census of Population and Housing: California), Table DP–1, pages 2, 20, 39, and 42. The fact that between 2002 and 2006 San Francisco lost more than 16,000 households with incomes of less than $150,000, while at the same time the city gained more than 17,000 households with incomes of more than $150,000 is shown on the front page of the June 22, 2008 issue of the *San Francisco Chronicle*, in an article titled "Exodus of S.F.'s Middle Class." The decline in school enrollment in the city of Palo Alto during the 1970s and the subsequent closing of several schools in that community were reported on page 90 of a 1982 study by the Stanford Environmental Law Society titled *Land Use and Housing on the San Francisco Peninsula*, edited by Thomas M. Hagler. Details on land use restrictions in Monterey County, California, are from pages A1 and A6 of the August 26–27, 2006 issue of the *Wall Street Journal*, under the headline "In Tony Monterey County, Slums and a Land War." The statement that trees take up more than six times as much space as all of the urban communities in the United States is from page 57 of *The Road More Traveled* by Ted Balaker and Sam Staley. The additional $100,000 or more in costs added to the price of homes in communities with "smart-growth" policies was noted on page 2 of "The Planning Penalty: How Smart Growth Makes Housing Unaffordable," written by Randal O'Toole and published by the Independent Institute in 2006.

CHAPTER 5: The Past and the Future

The quote "bad ages to live through are good ages to learn from" is from page 5 of *The Hollow Years: France in the 1930's* by Eugen Weber. Adam Smith's remarks about politicians can be found on page 435 of his *The Wealth of Nations*, Modern Library edition. The quote from the Soviet economists about the interconnected nature of prices is from page 172 of *The Turning Point*, by Nikolai Shmelev and Vladimir Popov. Hillary Clinton's calls for a tripling of the number of Section 8 housing vouchers and more public housing were reported on page B5 of the October 31, 2000 issue of the *New York Times*, under the title "Lazio Sought to Make a Legislative Mark in Housing." Senator Hillary Clinton's proposal to assist homeowners facing foreclosure was reported in an article from the August 18, 2007 *New York Times on the Web*, under the headline "Waking Up to the Real Estate Nightmare." That a higher share of homeowners than renters had housing costs exceeding 50% of household income in 2006 was shown on page 28 of *The State of the Nation's Housing 2008*, published by the Joint Center for Housing Studies of Harvard University in 2008. That a disproportionate share of the banks that failed during the Great Depression of the 1930s were in states with laws against branch banking was noted on pages 31, 55, and 58 of *FDR's Folly*, written by Jim Powell, while the statement that about 90 percent of these unit banks failed during the Great Depression can be found on the same pages. The fact that Canada experienced no bank failures during the Great Depression is from page 352 of *A Monetary History of the United States: 1867–1960*, written by Milton Friedman and Anna Jacobson Schwartz. The share of income required by American families to cover mortgage costs during the early 1980s, 1998 and 2005 was reported on page A1 of the December 29, 2005 issue of the *New York Times*, under the headline "Twenty Years Later, Buying a House Is Less of a Bite." That roughly 60% of first-time home buyers in Tucson relied on 100% financing to purchase a home in 2005 was reported on page D2 of the December 22, 2005 issue of the *Wall Street Journal*, in an article beginning on page D1 under the headline "Housing Affordability Hits 14-Year Low." The Republican proposal of granting government-backed, 4% fixed mortgages to credit-worthy borrowers was mentioned on page A13 of the February 5, 2009 issue of the *Wall Street Journal*, under the headline "The GOP Has a Dumb Mortgage Idea." Congressman Barney Frank's reference to Franklin D. Roosevelt is quoted from page A3 of the October 15, 2008 issue of the *Wall Street Journal*, in an article titled "Democrats Mull $300 Billion Stimulus." The claim that the New Deal "wasn't stimulative enough" is from the front page of the February 11, 2009 issue of the *Los Angeles Times*, under the headline "A Time for Boldness Beyond the

New Deal." Data showing that the annual unemployment rate exceeded 20% in the United States from 1932 through 1935 is shown on page 126 of Part 1 of *Historical Statistics of the United States: Colonial Times to 1970*, a publication of the U.S. Bureau of the Census published in 1975. Ways in which Franklin D. Roosevelt's New Deal policies were a further extension of the approach used by his predecessor, Herbert Hoover, are discussed on pages 148–149 of *The Forgotten Man*, written by Amity Shlaes and in Chapter 3 of *FDR's Folly* by Jim Powell. Walter Lippmann's remark that Roosevelt's New Deal was a "continuous evolution" of Hoover's measures is from page 757 of *A History of the American People*, written by Paul Johnson. President Hoover's recognition that his interventions in the economy were unprecedented is from page 29 of *The Memoirs of Herbert Hoover: The Great Depression, 1929–1941*. Data on page 77 of *Out of Work* by Richard Vedder and Lowell Gallaway show that the unemployment rate never fell below 20% during the first 21 months of FDR's administration. Additional information about unemployment rates in the wake of the October 1929 stock market crash and after the signing of the Smoot-Hawley tariffs are also from the same page. That FDR issued more executive orders during his administration than the combined total of all of his twentieth-century successors was reported on page xiii of *FDR's Folly* by Jim Powell. The concerns expressed by John Maynard Keynes about some of the New Deal reforms can be found on page xiv of the same book. That business investment remained low throughout the Great Depression is from page 161 of the same book. The statement that lending by banks during the 1930s was at about half the level of the 1920s is from page B5 of the January 27, 2009 issue of the *New York Times*, from an article beginning on page B1 under the headline "Something to Fear, After All." The fact that the unemployment rate never fell below the double-digit level for any year during FDR's first two terms in office is shown on page 77 of *Out of Work* by Richard Vedder and Lowell Gallaway. The study which concluded that the New Deal policies prevented a normal recovery in the economy and prolonged the Great Depression was published in the August 2004 issue of the *Journal of Political Economy*, in an article titled "New Deal Policies and the Persistence of the Great Depression: A General Equilibrium Analysis." Unemployment rates in the United States for the years 1937, 1940, 1941, 1942, and 1943–1945 are shown on page 126 of Part 1 of *Historical Statistics of the United States: Colonial Times to 1970*, a publication of the U.S. Bureau of the Census published in 1975. The federal deficit for the years 1936 and 1940 can be found on page 1105 of Part 2 of the same publication. FDR's discussion of "Dr. New Deal" and "Dr. Win-the-War" can be found on pages 569–571 of *The Public Papers and Addresses of Franklin D. Roosevelt: 1943 Volume*, published by Harper & Brothers. The decline in the velocity of the circulation of money during the Great Depression was discussed on pages 301–303 of *A Monetary History of the United States: 1867–1960* by Milton Friedman and Anna Jacobson Schwartz. Media criticisms of President Ronald Reagan for not intervening in the economy in the aftermath of the stock market crash of October 1987 can be found on page A35 of the October 22, 1987 issue of the *New York Times*, under the headline "Abroad at Home: It's Morning Again," on page A2 of the October 29, 1987 issue of the *Washington Post*, in an article titled "Fiddling While Wall St. Burns," and section 4, page 27 of the November 22, 1987 issue of the *New York Times*, in a column titled "Abroad at Home: Nobody at Home." The comments on 20 years of prosperity after 1987 from *The Economist* magazine are from page 35 of the September 22, 2007 issue, in an article titled "The Turning Point." The downturns in the economy during the 1920s that were left to recover on their own are mentioned on page 745 of the essay "Banking and Finance in the Twentieth Century," written by Eugene N. White and published in *The Cambridge Economic History of the United States, Volume 3: The Twentieth Century*, edited by Stanley L. Engerman and Robert E. Gallman. The comments from J.A. Schumpeter on non-intervention in an economy during a downturn are from page 110 of his essay "Depressions: Can We Learn from Past Experience?" in *Essays of J.A. Schumpeter*, edited by Richard V. Clemence. Karl Marx's remark about "crackbrained meddling by the authorities" is from his letter to Friedrich Engels dated February 3, 1851 and reprinted on page 275 of Volume 38 of their *Collected Works* in the edition published in Moscow in 1982. Walter Lippmann's comments about the goals of the New Deal were quoted on page xv of *FDR's Folly* by Jim Powell. That many of the decision makers of the New Deal administration were advocates of government intervention and in favor of restructuring the economy, even before the stock market crash of 1929 and the Great Depression, is discussed on pages 3, 10, and 15 of *FDR's Folly* by Jim Powell, and also pages 53–56 and 64–69 of *The Forgotten Man* by Amity Shlaes. Professor Alan Blinder's comments on the stimulus bill of 2009 are from page A13 of the February 4, 2009 issue of the *Wall Street Journal*, under the headline "My Economic Wish List." Rahm Emanuel's remarks about crisis as an opportunity not to be "wasted" were quoted on page 25 of the February 1, 2009 issue of *New York Times Magazine*, in an article titled "The Big Fix." That lending money to home buyers had been a highly profitable and low risk endeavor for banks for nearly a century was stated on page 1 of *Financial Shock* by Mark Zandi. The growing demands placed on banks receiving government bailout money were described on the front page of the March 11, 2009 issue of the *New York Times*, under the headline "Some Banks, Feeling Chained, Want to Return Bailout Money." Paul Johnson's quote can be found on page 138 of *The Quotable Paul Johnson* edited by George J. Marlin, et al.

INDEX